Advance Praise for *Love in a F*cked-Up World*

"Dean Spade's *Love in a F*cked-Up World* is a revolutionary guide for navigating relationships in these challenging times. With unflinching honesty and radical compassion, Spade offers invaluable insights into how dominant cultural scripts shape our connections, providing practical tools for breaking free from harmful relational patterns. I highly recommend this book for anyone seeking to build more authentic, liberating relationships while dismantling oppressive systems. As someone deeply invested in helping people create secure attachments in nontraditional relationships, I'm thrilled to see Spade's intersectional, justice-oriented approach to love and intimacy. This work has the power to transform not just our personal lives but our communities and movements as well."

—JESSICA FERN, author of *Polysecure* and *Polywise*

"Dean Spade has written a pragmatic, timely book to help us navigate our most intimate relationships with a collective mind-set; release romance myths and approach love as a practice; and cultivate discernment and freedom where we are trained toward judgment and ownership. He teaches us with gentle, relatable clarity and questions that allow us to reflect on how we are loving each other in this fucked-up, gorgeous world, and how to hold on to each other as the changes come."

—ADRIENNE MAREE BROWN, author of *Loving Corrections,*
Pleasure Activism, and *Emergent Strategy*

"Against the backdrop of societ~~al~~
*F*cked-Up World* offers a beauti
how to cultivate relationships t

D1707453

also revolutionary, that change our world—and ultimately our earth—at its root. Drawing on decades of leadership in social movements, Dean Spade inextricably links personal healing with collective liberation, encouraging readers to rethink the ways we connect, love, and resist in an increasingly complex world."

—TOURMALINE, co-editor of *Trap Door: Trans Cultural Production and the Politics of Visibility*

"Compassionate, clarifying, and profoundly wise, *Love in a F*cked-Up World* is radical leftist thought leader Dean Spade's latest gift to anyone interested in the intersection of love and justice…In this clear and highly practical book, Spade offers an enormously helpful map for creating relationships—whether friendly, sexual, and/or romantic—that feed and strengthen not only the individuals involved but their communities and social commitments as well…This is the book I desperately needed when I first joined social justice movements as a teenager, and I am so very grateful that activists of all ages may read it now."

—KAI CHENG THOM, author of *Falling Back in Love with Being Human: Letters to Lost Souls*

"As a politicized person and a queer therapist, I have long wished for more self-help literature that is collectivist, anticapitalist, and grounded in radical tradition. Dean Spade's *Love in a F*cked-Up World* nails it; a loving and fearless book full of rigor, candor, and wisdom from someone who has lived a life devoted to activist community."

—HANNAH BAER, therapist and author of *Trans Girl Suicide Museum*

love in a
f*cked-up world

love in a
f*cked-up world

how to build relationships,
hook up, and raise hell together

DEAN SPADE

ALGONQUIN BOOKS OF CHAPEL HILL   2025

Published by
ALGONQUIN BOOKS OF CHAPEL HILL
an imprint of Little, Brown and Company
a division of Hachette Book Group, Inc.
1290 Avenue of the Americas
New York, NY 10104

The Algonquin Books of Chapel Hill name and logo are registered
trademarks of Hachette Book Group, Inc.

Design by Steve Godwin.

The publisher is not responsible for websites (or their content)
that are not owned by the publisher.

Library of Congress Cataloging-in-Publication Data is available.

ISBN 978-1-64375-646-2 (paperback)
ISBN 978-1-64375-647-9 (ebook)

10 9 8 7 6 5 4 3 2 1
First Edition

For lovers and fighters

contents

4 Encountering Fear, and the Courage to Say Yes and No

introduction

Everything worthwhile is done with other people.
—MARIAME KABA, *We Do This 'Til We Free Us*

An increase in the capacity to affect and be affected—joy—
means being more in touch with a world that is bleeding,
burning, screaming.... Freedom [is] not the absence of
constraint or a do-what-you-like individualism but an
emergent capacity to work on relationships, shift desires,
and undo ingrained habits.
—CARLA BERGMAN AND NICK MONTGOMERY,
*Joyful Militancy: Building Thriving Resistance
in Toxic Times*

FOR TWO DECADES, I have been part of social movements
striving to end criminalization and violence and build a world
where all people have what they need. I have been a lawyer,
writer, and organizer in the trans liberation, anti-war, and
prison abolition movements. This work in resistance movements has been the biggest joy of my life and the source of my
deepest friendships. The conditions under which we now live
are brutal, but I find inspiration and strength in studying and

being part of the resistance, working side by side with people who have devoted their lives to liberation.

But resistance movements are also sites of intense conflict—certainly with the powers that be, but just as often within movements themselves. Revolutionary energy creates a charged atmosphere both politically and personally. Conflicts that are simultaneously about what we should do together and about our personality differences often get in the way of the work.

It's not surprising that friendships and sexual relationships develop between organizers, where passions run high, and shared values and goals give a sense of belonging or intimacy. Of course we're going to hook up with the hot, brilliant people in our movements—those who understand our ideas and want to fight for liberation. As a feminist and a queer, I know how important sexuality can be as a site of transformation, expression, and community-building. Sexual and romantic relationships are thrilling, and can be meaningful sites of self-discovery, support, and healing. In fact, many people join resistance movements to find like-minded people. It might be obvious to say that sex and other types of connection go hand in hand with resistance work—we find the relationships we've longed for in resistance movements.

But the excitement of finding these intense connections doesn't guarantee that they will unfold smoothly. Working day to day with others in these movements, I have seen and experienced too often how difficult and destructive relationship conflict between organizers can be. Even people who have dedicated their lives to their principles can end up acting in unprincipled ways, often unconsciously, in relationships.

Why is it that we find the courage to boldly confront mainstream societal norms and structures, yet are so often unable to treat romantic partners with care and generosity? Why do we lose our principles when we become insecure, disappointed, or jealous? Why do we act our worst in sexual and romantic relationships? And why do we prioritize romantic connection above other types of relationships, like friendship?

I have seen again and again how difficult it is for us to align our values with our actions in relationships. I've witnessed first-hand the way our behavior with romantic and sexual partners can explode groups, sabotage projects, and thwart our work. I have deeply questioned my own behavior, used countless tools to make changes, and helped those I mentor and collaborate with to transform these harmful patterns in themselves.

I wrote this book because the stakes are extremely high: I believe we *can* and *must* bring our most radical, visionary ideas of liberation into our practices of sex, love, and romance, and to all the relationships in our lives. We need each other now more than ever, and we have to learn how to stick together, even when emotions run hot. *Love in a Fucked-Up World* doesn't offer a quick fix or thirty-day solution. Those don't happen in real life. What it does offer is a practical road-map for how to navigate some of the most common patterns of relationship conflict, and practical tools for managing knee-jerk reactions in situations of high emotion. This book can help you build the liberatory, supportive relationships you crave, and strengthen the groups and movements you care about.

To bring our principles more fully into our relationships, we need to:

1   Understand the cultural messages and conditioning that dictate our ideas of what relationships should be.

2   Identify the way those conditions and cultural "scripts" influence our own behavior and reactions.

3   Take practical steps to deescalate our knee-jerk, or "conditioned" reactions, and move toward behavior that aligns with our beliefs about how we want to treat ourselves and others.

Throughout this book, I will share stories drawn from my life, as well as from the lives of people I collaborate with in movements, stories about struggling with the range of relationship tangles that haunt so many of us. I'll also offer questions and exercises to help you dig into how harmful cultural narratives might be impacting your own expectations and communication in relationships. These exercises are the first step to getting free from cultural conditioning.

THE FAMOUS FEMINIST slogan "the personal is political" is correct: it matters what happens in our intimate lives. Our romantic lives are not just some private thing that we're failing or succeeding at. When it comes to sex, love and romance, each of us is under pressure from cultural norms, and each of us needs support to unlearn messed-up ideas and behaviors. Through sex, romance, love, and friendship, we can cultivate new experiences of liberation and pleasure. We all want to feel truly seen and cared for, to feel connected and loved, to experience pleasure and creativity, and to do this we need to bring our best thinking about freedom and justice into alignment with our desires for healing and connection.

My previous books might seem quite different from this one. My first book, *Normal Life: Administrative Violence, Critical Trans Politics and the Limits of Law*, addresses how targeted groups have borne the brunt of changes to welfare, immigration, policing, and healthcare, and explores how resistance movements, especially the fight for trans liberation, can avoid getting co-opted and thwarted. My second book, *Mutual Aid: Building Solidarity During This Crisis (and the Next)*, looks at how we can work together effectively in mutual aid groups to respond to crises ourselves, rather than begging for change from governments or corporations. To me, *Love in a Fucked-Up World* is a clear extension of the questions at the heart of my previous work: How do we build lasting and effective resistance movements? What are the barriers impeding our movements, and how do we overcome them? This book adds another, very human, layer to that project—in the form of a self-help guide to sex, love, romance, and friendship.

The mainstream relationship self-help literature can take us only so far. There are books that offer good insights about specific patterns and behaviors, but almost all retain outdated, often sexist, ideas about sex and romance. There are very few that do not focus on white, straight, upper-class people's lives, which limits their relevance, particularly to people in resistance movements.

Most love and romance self-help books are written by therapists and based on their sessions with individuals and couples. Or else by someone who claims to be extremely savvy about dating or communication. I'm a lawyer, professor, and activist, and no one familiar with my dating history would accuse me of having it all figured out. But I'm a longtime participant in and student of social movements, and for twenty-five years, I've been relentlessly working to improve my relationships.

The most profound insights I've encountered about how to treat each other in relationships come from writers like Audre Lorde, bell hooks, Lauren Berlant, Emi Koyama, Shira Hassan, and Mariame Kaba: people whose wisdom about relationships comes from being part of communities in crisis and movements for justice. This is not an accident. This book is by, for, and about people who are motivated to collectively resist normative cultural expectations, one relationship at a time. And to do that, we have to look inward and unlearn the cultural messaging that is drilled into us from an early age.

When it comes to sex, love and friendship, one of the most damaging cultural narratives—or "scripts," as I refer to them in this book—is the *romance myth*. The romance myth tells us that romantic relationships are the most important relationships in our lives and that they are the place where we become complete, satisfied, loved, and safe.

Surveys in the US and Canada have shown that people now rate love as their number one goal in life, over financial success or a satisfying career. People today rank love as more important than anything else in their relationships. Compare that to the 1930s, when love was ranked fifth, after qualities like dependable character, emotional maturity, and pleasing disposition. More than ever, people expect to get their needs for intimacy and security met in their romantic partnerships. Romantic "love"—through the influence of movies, advertising, and TV shows—has become a catchall for having all our emotional, sexual, and companionship needs met. This privileging of romantic love (above all else) encourages people to disregard friendship when love comes calling, and it cultivates insecurity, desperation, and competition about sex and romance.

The romance myth tells us that romance is eternal and exclusive, and that to be loved (or to love) means belonging to (or owning) someone. It tells us that there is something wrong with us, our love, or our partner if we have different needs or wants, because true love is easy, natural, and unchanging.

When I say it this bluntly, we can see how these messages are inaccurate and damaging. We can see how, under the influence of this myth, romantic love might follow a predictable cycle, starting with intoxicating intensity then moving into a conflict phase characterized by disappointment and resentment. We can see how possession and ownership models lead to harmful, controlling behaviors. In short, we see our friends—and ourselves—fuck up our lives and hurt each other, making bad decisions driven by illusions about romantic relationships.

Yet most of us are still haunted by the romance myth. When things don't work out with a date, we see it as our own failure. We assume it was our fault, that we chose the wrong person, and that if we just choose better the next time, we'll break out of the cycle. We judge and blame our exes and speak badly of them in our communities. Or we judge ourselves harshly because we don't have specifically romantic relationships, discounting the importance of friendship and other connections in our lives. This is just one of the ways cultural scripts alter our expectations and behavior and fundamentally undermine our efforts to build satisfying, inspiring, ethical relationships.

This book dares us to decide that romance is not separate from our politics of liberation and resistance. Relationships are a place where we can practice our principles and values, rather than acting out messed-up cultural scripts fed to us by corporate media. If we want to build a world organized around care, connection, and freedom, we must combine our work "out there" with rigorous work in our intimate lives. We need each other so badly right now. We must learn how to come together in love and resistance in this fucked-up world.

This book is for you if you:

* Keep having the same breakup over and over.
* Can't stop obsessively checking your dating apps, but also feel exhausted, bored, and defeated about the lack of options.
* Can't rely on your friend circle because of friendship and romantic turmoil, friends disappearing because of new romances or taking sides in breakups and dividing the group.
* Feel isolated in your love relationship and wish you had more close friends.

* Got hurt by someone and now are on a campaign to make other people break ties with that person, leaving lots of wreckage in your wake.
* Pine for the perfect romance, job, or body, thinking that would fix everything.
* Are trying to be perfect and feel deflated or defensive when you get critical feedback, or are so scared of negative feedback that you don't risk trying new things.
* Can't stop taking care of everyone around you, can't figure out how to say no, and are resentful and tired.
* Can't figure out how to say yes to friendship, dating, and/or other relationships, and keep pushing people away even though you don't want to.
* Often think, "I hate people." You believe in compassion, connection, and collective action in the abstract, but you are tired of how annoying people are.
* Are weary of constant conflict in activist groups and feel hopeless about joining new efforts, even though you want to be part of collective action for change.

Dominant Culture's Scripts Are Still Shaping Our Relationships

I'm not saying it don't hurt to be awake in this world.
But stay awake my darlings.
—MARSHA P JOHNSON [1]

I trace the curve of your jaw
with a lover's finger
knowing the hardest battle
is only the first
how to do what we need for our living
with honour and in love
we have chosen each other
and the edge of each other's battles
the war is the same . . .
—AUDRE LORDE

MAINSTREAM CULTURE BOMBARDS us with images of romantic love as the key to happiness. Many people have, or hope for, thrilling sexual and romantic experiences that bring excitement, pleasure, and a powerful sense of being cared for and accepted into their lives. At the same time, most of us have also noticed that people act their very worst toward their lovers, and often sacrifice other relationships and priorities in pursuit of romantic connections. Worse, we are pushed to believe that the issues that inevitably emerge in our relationships are the result of our shortcomings or those of our friends, lovers, or partners. Rarely do we imagine that our relationship troubles originate with, and are in service to, powerful systems of domination and control. Intimate partner violence occurs in 30 percent of romantic relationships—queer and straight—and plenty more relationships foster emotional dynamics that cause people to feel isolated, afraid, bored, unloved, anxious, or trapped.

Even before the COVID-19 pandemic, long work hours, commuting, moving away from home for jobs and school, and spending more time online, have increased isolation across demographics. Since COVID-19 that isolation has only worsened, as have rising costs of food and rent, deepening debt, and growing inequality. More people are living alone, and many have fewer close relationships. These factors combine with the romance myth to create the feeling that a romantic partner *can and should* meet all our emotional needs. We're taught to find a partner to fill the chasm created by these impossible conditions.

Of course, no one person can or should meet all of another's needs. Too often, we do not have robust support systems to turn to for perspective and help when relationships get hard. And many of us who are not in relationships get caught in an unfulfilling obsession with online dating, often spending countless hours on the apps hoping to find satisfaction, sometimes with unrealistic expectations.

We have all seen friends hurt by romantic partners. We have all seen one another drop out of groups and activities we care about because of new love or relationship drama. We have seen friend groups, activist collectives, workplaces, and artistic collaborations torn apart by conflict related to sex and romance. And we have felt the pain of being stuck in our own difficult relationship dynamics.

With so many of us trapped in these stressful, demoralizing, and demobilizing situations, how are we supposed to get together to try to overturn the dominant systems that are hurting so many people and destroying the planet? In order to break the cycles of heartbreak, jealousy, possessiveness, boredom, numbness, conflict, isolation, and betrayal, we need to understand the larger social dynamics that often guide our behavior and desires.

Mainstream ideas about romance and sex perpetuate systems of domination, reinforcing ideas of what relationship should look and feel like. They teach us what to want. They tell us that certain things, like being skinny, rich, or married, will make us happy and fulfilled. Those beliefs—even when we *intellectually* understand them to be distortions—impact our feelings and behavior. What do they do to our ability to thrive together? How do we get out from under their control?

It's easier to identify the way cultural scripts influence our desires to buy stuff. Our friend groups or subcultures might encourage us to divest from gas-guzzling cars, blood diamonds, or sweatshop-made clothes. But powerful cultural scripts also often determine what we want when it comes to sex and romance. We are taught that relationships should be exclusive, long-lasting, and follow a predetermined pattern of escalation. But just as with toxic commodities, these societally prescribed guidelines are destructive. When we mistake these cultural messages as our own feelings and desires, our relationships follow damaging patterns set up for us by dominant culture.

We often treat overwhelming feelings—like jealousy, loneliness, obsession—as natural, inevitable, or irresistible. We may not even realize we are under the control of myths about sex and romance, because they feel so personal. They feel like they originate *inside* us, but the seeds were planted by the dominant culture's messages. We have to unlearn this conditioning in order to find more supportive and transformative ways to desire and be with one another.

In this chapter, we'll take a close look at some of the cultural scripts that shape our feelings and behaviors in relationships. Understanding how our feelings are shaped by this cultural conditioning, and the difficulties it creates, can help us break free. We'll dig into several practice exercises for noticing and beginning to liberate ourselves from their thrall so we can make the connections we want and need.

Yikes! You are reading a self-help book. You may be thinking:

* I don't have time for this.
* I'm scared to look at my feelings.
* If I dig into my past, I won't be able to function.
* I'm scared to change anything in my life.
* If I bring up my concerns, I will lose my relationship(s).
* I'm scared no one will like the real self I would have to face.
* This stuff is cheesy/neoliberal/woo woo.
* These things are for weak people.
* This individualistic "self-help" shit is liberal, bougie, and a distraction from collective action.

These are common feelings that come up for many people thinking about going to therapy, reading a self-help book, or doing other stuff that might dig into emotions, patterns, and reactions. You can notice those feelings and keep reading anyway. You can ask yourself where those ideas came from—is there someone's voice you hear in your head? If so, is that a person you want to be guided by? You can remind yourself that reading this book won't cause anything to spiral out of control—you will still get to choose what you do with what you read. You can remind yourself why you picked up this book in the first place: Are there things going on in your life that you want to change that have something to do with how you feel or react in relationships? Can you identify ways in which improving your relational skills would help you show up in resistance movements more effectively? Remembering your motivation can help if discouraging thoughts emerge. You can also set up a support plan. Is there a friend you can check in with as you read? Can you go at a slow pace? Can you do nice things for yourself that help you relax while you read? There is no rush to read this or to do anything in particular with what you learn. Being curious is enough.

Feeling Bad While Things Are Bad

WE LIVE IN a time of intense conditions. We are told we are freer and more connected than ever because of technology, but every day we confront skyrocketing inequality, terrifying ecological crisis, and endless war. Many of us are fed up and want change, and are working together to fight back. But at the same time, it can feel as though we are all just having fights online while everything in the real world gets worse. Many people feel powerless, unable to imagine a world not defined by greed, hierarchy, and exploitation. At the same time, we are inundated with new ways to distract ourselves and numb out with screens, which can exacerbate our disconnection from each other and the natural world. To cope, we are pushed to consume things that help us feel good(ish) in the short term but often lead to long-term imbalances in our bodies and minds, and contribute to our isolation.

Humans evolved in groups, sharing everything in order to survive. We are built to connect and relate. Caring for one another and working to make things better fills our lives with meaning, satisfaction, creativity, joy, and a sense of belonging. Having close relationships and people to rely on can make the difference between being safe and unsafe in a crisis, or even getting by at all. The systems we live under tell us that being rich, being "fit," having an elite job, owning the right things, or getting married will make us happy. They train us to treat each other as disposable and to measure ourselves against hierarchies that make us feel unworthy. Our relationships to those around us are what make up our worlds; they comprise *the* world. We need to liberate them.

Humans are relational: we need each other. We cannot survive alone, and whether or not we acknowledge that interdependency, it determines everything about our lives.

Cultural fantasies about "independent individuals" hide our essential reliance on one another, discounting and minimizing the care work (cleaning, cooking, looking after children and elders, emotional support) that makes our lives happen. Racial capitalism—the global system of racial exploitation that fuels the unbridled accumulation of wealth by the few and the suffering of the many—teaches us to think of ourselves as individuals, competing for what we can get at each other's expense.

If we break the illusion of separateness, we can see that we already exist in a web of mutual care necessary for us to survive—we get everything we need from each other and the planet. It's just that this web is mediated by violence and coercion so that a few people can profit. Our job is to resist and destroy the systems that turn our lives into fuel for exploiting, planet-destroying industries. We must both invent new and restore old ways of living with each other, ways that nurture life, connection, belonging, and liberation. From the day we are born, those skills are undermined and sabotaged by cultural messaging. We're taught to be competitive, individualistic, acquisitive, and hierarchical.

What if, when we encountered conflict, we didn't have to try to figure out who was in the wrong? What if we expected that conflict would be a predictable and generative part of any relationship? What if we all had enough support from friends that we could weather the storm of a conflict or breakup?

What if we were so good at giving and receiving feedback along the way that our relationships didn't frequently devolve into resentment or blow up in dramatic endings?

Given the circumstances of the world we live in, it makes sense for us to feel afraid and overwhelmed. How can we hold on to each other in these hard times, take the brave and bold actions required of us, and become better able to love each other through it all? If we're going to stick together through this, we have to shake off the constricting conditioning we have received about love and relationships.

- * What have you seen cause conflict and disconnection in your friend circles or communities?
- * Can you imagine, or have you experienced, difference and conflict in relationships generating *more* connection, belonging, autonomy, and creativity rather than less? What supports that?

Breaking Ties with Tired Cultural Scripts

IF WE WANT liberation, we need to be able to see things as they really are. Cultural forces—sexism, racism, capitalism, and colonialism—distort our perceptions like a prism splinters light, causing us to see skewed visions of ourselves and those around us. Scripts are implanted in our psyches through relentless repetition. We then go through life on *autopilot*, acting out these scripts without thinking about it consciously. This idea of autopilot means that many of our responses, behaviors, and even feelings aren't really *ours*. They have been programmed into us, and we unknowingly parrot them.

When we are on autopilot, we don't question our assumptions or our knee-jerk reactions; we don't notice that our behaviors are less likely to match up with our principles. One effect of autopilot is that we are often drawn into polarized thinking. We lose nuance and complexity, thinking in extremes like "I'm the worst!" "I can't do this!" "It's her fault!" "This can never work!" "This always happens!"

Throughout this book, we will use the image of a pendulum (like the one below) to explore how those extreme, often polarized thoughts emerge when we are in a reactive or fearful state. The goal is to get enough critical distance from this reactive thinking so we can break the hold it has on us when we are stirred up. The pendulum image below explores a common reactive polarity: thinking that we are the best or the worst. Neither is likely true, but it can be easy to flip into one or the other when we get riled up.

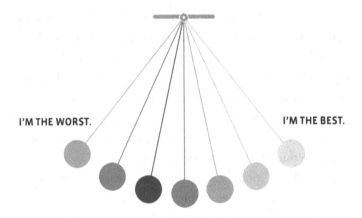

Because we live in a society that pushes blame, punishment, and hierarchy, most of us swing between these poles whenever we encounter a conflict. If we can observe that something is off—that our perception of reality is distorted—when we are thinking "I'm the worst," we might realize we want to seek help or a new perspective. If we don't notice, we might cause harm to ourself or others. For example, we might start to believe we're always the victim. This can make us feel entitled to lash out, or to ignore other people's feedback about how our actions affect them. Shame from believing we are the worst can, ironically, make us unable to listen to people close to us and respond to their requests, because we are stuck in thinking about how bad we are. If we can start to notice when "I'm the worst" comes into our minds, we can break out of its hold and not follow its scripts.

"I'm the best!" can feel pretty good. But it can cause us to incorrectly assume someone else is in the wrong, or cause us to feel certain that we know what is best for others. In both instances, we're not listening carefully. We may become impermeable and rigid in our opinions, undermining our connections to others.

When we find ourselves in those extremes, unable to perceive the nuances of a situation, we are usually in a state of fear-based conditioning, something that generates significant conflict and hurt in relationships. Remembering a phrase like "I'm not the best, I'm not the worst" while sorting through an emotionally charged situation can help us find counterevidence to our most reactive self-narratives, and move toward a more solid basis for taking action.

Identifying the conditioned habits that get in the way of our liberation can help us build awareness for the times when these distortions have us in their clutches. Exploring some commonly internalized cultural scripts that cause us to act out, on autopilot, can help us make conscious choices about our behavior in relationships.

I'm Not Saying It's All in Your Head

The worst thing about self-help tools is that most of them make it seem like, no matter what problems you're having, you just have to change yourself, your thinking, your attitude, and then it will all get better. This is nonsense. There are real, awful conditions we live under, and the way out of them is collective action to destroy racial capitalism, patriarchy, and colonialism. At the same time, it's true that this stuff gets in our heads. We are raised to act out its designs, to become people who could abuse, dominate, and cage others. We are brainwashed to become complacent with our own or others' subjugation. As a result, we need to do work simultaneously both inside ourselves and against our oppressors.

Ableism, ageism, racism, gender norm enforcement, and fat shaming play a huge role in creating isolation for many people. They cause us to devalue one another and paint specific bodies as undesirable. I take seriously how much those norms determine many people's access to sex, love, companionship, and friendship. We must collectively transform our friend circles, social scenes, and subcultures, upending these cruel hierarchies of desirability.

TV shows, movies, and messages from our families, friends, and communities all tell us that romantic love is central to our lives and the key to happiness. However, romantic love has not always been the basis for forming families or even making choices about sexual partners. It has a history of invention and deployment, just like other harmful structures that have been portrayed as natural and universal, such as white supremacy and Manifest Destiny.

The idea of romance is culturally specific, hasn't always existed, and has changed over time. Most people across history organized communal care, tending to illness and child-rearing outside the confines of marriage or monogamy. Sexual expression has had extraordinarily diverse manifestations across time and geography. Even in an industrial consumer society such as the US, where I live, research shows there used to be less expectation for needs to be met through romantic relationships than there is now. As we face surging isolation, reduced friendship, and vanishing intracommunity support, we are pushed to rely on a romantic relationship for every kind of care we need.

The current norm, the nuclear family, emerged to replace larger family groups doing subsistence agriculture, as capitalism required more mobile industrial and service wage-workers. Romantic love became one of the social structures that keeps us in our places in a system designed to extract from workers and the planet to make a small number of people very rich. Systems of taxation, property, healthcare, housing, and immigration are all now designed around the marital family unit. Whether or not we organize our lives that way, that norm is the current blueprint. We are told it is "natural," when in fact it's just a particular design that is currently dominant. In that way, our ideas about sex and romance are a product of racial capitalism, but they feel quite personal. The process of liberating our relationships requires us to realize that these desires didn't come from inside us, and that we can choose what to cultivate and pursue.

Central Lies of the Romance Myth

* A committed romantic/sexual relationship is the most important kind of relationship.
* There is something wrong with you if you aren't in one, and you have less value.
* Real love lasts forever.
* The right relationship will make you happy.

The romance myth tells us that there is one true love out there for each of us. It says that if you find—and keep—the right person, sex and love will flow easily, perpetually, and naturally. This myth insists you will not be attracted to other people, and you will consistently feel love and sexual attraction for each other. It teaches that romantic partners should take a set of escalating steps together from the outset of their relationship: agreeing to be sexually exclusive, moving in together, making a lifelong commitment, merging financial lives, and having children. If someone doesn't want those things, then there must be something wrong with them. Or they aren't truly in love, or maybe they're just being selfish. The romance myth says that if your love is real, you can and should give up anything for the other person.

The romance myth also teaches us that everyone should compete for the best possible partners. "Best" is defined by racial, economic, gender, health, and body-shape norms. Dating is a competitive market; therefore you make sure to get the best possible mate for your long-term commitment, "trading up" whenever possible. We are all supposed to fear being alone, being left, or getting stuck with a "loser" for a partner. Thus, we see one another through a calculating view of appraisal and competition, in which everyone vies for the "best" partners based on criteria rooted in oppressive norms. This leads to dehumanization, in which we evaluate each other like commodities, and some people are marked as undesirable.

The Transformative Power of Love?

This book has such a critical take on romance and love that you might wonder, what about the transformative power of love? Living in a society that is under the spell of the romance myth, we constantly hear overblown promises about how love will complete us, so I won't focus on that in this book. However, I do think that sexual and romantic relationships, because they stir up such strong reactions in us, can be profound places to learn about our wounds and cultural conditioning, and to experience connections that heal.

My sister once told me that caramel is the most dangerous thing in the kitchen. It gets so hot, it's incredibly easy to get horrible burns. Sexual and romantic relationships, similarly, are wildly sweet, and risky. So many risky things are worth it: changing your gender, leaving your abusive family or religious community, defending your friends from cops, blocking coal trains and oil pipelines, squatting, taking over your campus, breaking rules, making art.

This book is pro-risk, pro-sex, and pro-love of all kinds, but it also asks you to take an unflinching look at how our behavior in sexual and romantic relationships often hurts us, hurts others, and impacts our social movement efforts. I hope what's here helps you find ways to have all the liberated pleasure you want. I hope we all feel the love of solidarity, of care for the vulnerable, of bold action with friends and strangers, of being connected to the living Earth, of breaking captivity together.

How Does the Romance Myth Mess Up Our Relationships?

BECAUSE THE ROMANCE myth implies that everyone should follow the same prescribed steps to achieve love and satisfaction, it causes us to make assumptions about others' wants and needs. It makes us assume our partners' sexual, social, or other needs will be "normal"—either just like our own, or like what we have interpreted as normal from mainstream scripts. It leads us to judge ourselves and each other negatively if we don't want what we are told is "normal"—for example, if someone wants to live alone through adulthood, or wants to have sex less or more than they are "supposed to," or doesn't desire marriage.

The romance myth causes many people to make big life decisions without adequate reflection, like moving far away for a partner's work, leaving friends and community behind. It causes us to underinvest in our friendships and other support circles, to prioritize lovers over friends, which often leads to isolation. The romance myth asks us to "give up" parts of ourselves in the name of love, often leaving us less prepared or supported to deal with life's challenges, including those that happen inside our romantic relationships. The romance myth also rationalizes jealousy and possessiveness in ways that can escalate conflict and even be used to justify abuse.

Under the influence of the romance myth, resentments fester, and we swerve into stagnated blame dynamics. "If you really loved me you would . . ."

* want to have sex when I do
* marry me
* move in together
* have a child with me
* give up an activity because I disapprove of it
* spend more time with me instead of with your friends or by yourself
* change a behavior because I don't like it
* accept a behavior of mine even though it hurts you
* spend time with my family even though they mistreat one or both of us

These examples of romance myth ideas surfacing in relationships could come up in the course of ordinary conflict. However, they could also be part of a pattern of abuse. Building awareness about how these ideas get in our heads and shape our expectations and demands in a relationship is useful for figuring out what we really want. But it will not resolve a pattern of abuse.

Distinguishing Conflict and Abuse

There is no single perfect definition of the difference between conflict and abuse, but wise people from the antiviolence movement have long asserted that abusive relationships include one person trying to maintain control over someone else in a repeated pattern, and refusing to take responsibility for the harm they cause. We all feel urges to control others sometimes, and we all cause hurt and harm to others at times. But abuse occurs during a more sustained pattern of uneven power, control, and mistreatment. When a person is enacting or experiencing abuse, the situation calls for firmer boundaries and more support than one might need in dealing with nonabusive conflict.

Distinguishing conflict from abuse is difficult, and the stakes are high. As Weyam Ghadbian, a facilitator specializing in conflict mediation, says, "People try to minimize abuse by characterizing it as conflict and overblow conflict by characterizing it as abuse." Jovida Ross, another conflict facilitation expert, observes that "approaching abuse as conflict is a setup for more abuse, and mischaracterizing conflict as abuse can itself be a move to exert control." This book cannot resolve this challenge, but hopefully it will provide tools to help us better understand our own experiences and impacts on others and build relationships based on consent. If you are trying to figure out whether your relationship is abusive, it is essential to reach out for support: you can talk to friends, work with a therapist, or call a hotline. Some resources include: The Network/La Red, (800) 832-1901; A Call for Change, (877) 898-3411; the Northwest Network, (206) 568-7777; and API Chaya, (877) 922-4292.

The Truth About Love

THE TRUTH IS, no one person can meet every emotional need we have. We are safer and better off with more kinds of connection, are more able to survive and resist with creativity and stamina when we cultivate trust and connectedness with many people. There is no "normal" way of being or relating. If we want people to understand what we want and how we want to be treated, we have to tell them. They can say "yes" or "no" to our requests, and if they say "no," we can seek to get our needs met elsewhere, meet the needs ourselves, or live without them being met.

Despite strong messages from mainstream culture, there is no "natural" way to experience romance or sex. Even sustained, fun, mutual, pleasurable sexual relationships require negotiation and renegotiation and will go through ebbs and flows. Change is inevitable, change is not a betrayal. Similarly, despite the heavy pressure of monogamous norms, the truth is that being attracted to someone else besides your partner, even strongly, does not mean there is something wrong with your relationship.

At the same time, strong attraction to a new person does not mean that we have no choice but to pursue them, or that they are our destiny. A new attraction does not justify dishonesty. Committed relationships, polyamorous relationships, friends with benefits, monogamous relationships, hookups and anonymous sex, brief relationships, and open relationships are all politically and morally equal. There is not a better or worse, or more radical, form for sexual or romantic connection. Hierarchies of value regarding types of relationships generally obstruct people's self-determination and perpetuate patterns of shame, betrayal, dishonesty, disconnection, and discontent.

The truth is that there is no relationship that will automatically make you happy. We will bring our long-term emotional patterns and settings into every relationship we enter. We're still us, even in a different relationship. Romantic and sexual relationships can be a place to learn about ourselves and grow, particularly as they stir up strong, complex feelings and often stimulate wounds from our childhoods or families of origin. But they are not more necessary or important than other relationships.

The good feelings of a new crush don't just come from the other person, they spring from our own capacities for connection, joy, pleasure, creativity, and excitement. We can and should bring those capacities into all kinds of relationships and activities, not just romantic ones.

Despite the romance myth's insistence on duration, it is neither better nor worse to stay in a relationship or to break up. Both are opportunities for growth. Efforts to own or control other people, or to control other people's thoughts and emotions, are futile and painful. Compromising ourselves and stifling our desires generates resentment and contempt.

At their best, our relationships support our full development, and cultivate our desires rather than treating them as threats.

The romance myth tells us that there is a scarcity of partners, a more valuable partner just around the corner, or only one right person for each of us. Such scarcity thinking serves consumer culture's constant drive to make us feel inadequate, and can also make people stay in unworkable relationships. We live in a world of social possibility, and while there are real ways that racism, fat shaming, misogyny, gender binarism, classism, ageism, geography, language, and ableism impact sex and dating pools, the scarcity framework will not help us resist those oppressions together. Needs associated with romantic relationships—such as sexual gratification, physical affection, affirmation, play, companionship, sharing meals, and cohabitation—can also be met through friendships, family, and/or through our relationship with ourselves. In fact, as I will discuss later, joining resistance groups, while not always easy, is a gorgeous way to find your people.

Marriage Isn't Love or Liberation

BY DEFINITION, COUNTERCULTURAL movements like feminism, Black liberation, and queer liberation question the dominant culture, including its scripts about what is beautiful and desirable or taboo, as well as about how people should relate to each other and form families. In the sixties, seventies, and eighties,[2] feminists and queers broke the silence about domestic violence and child sexual abuse, exposing marriage as a form of social control and the family as a site of violence against women and children. They worked to make it easier to get divorced and challenged legal structures that stigmatized children born out of wedlock. They exposed and debunked racist ideas that attributed poverty in Black communities to low marriage rates.[3] Throughout the feminist and antiracist movements of the sixties and seventies, young people created subcultures that celebrated casual sex, public sex, nonprocreative sex, gay sex, single parenthood, nonmarital cohabitation, alternative family structures, kink, friendship, communities of care, and female sexual pleasure. Central to these efforts was a critique of marriage as a form of control over women, a vehicle for consolidating wealth, and a system that rewarded conformity with the government's family-formation norms.

In the 1980s, however, there was a backlash against these emancipating ideas. Dominant systems coopted feminist and queer symbols and concepts, evacuating their radical potential and selling an empty version back to us as "liberation." In the 1990s and 2000s, a new set of nonprofits led by white lawyers undertook same-sex marriage advocacy, portraying marriage as a site of love and connection despite its obvious role as a structure of state control. Marriage was reframed as something that gay people wanted to be included in rather than help destroy. Instead of queers being a threat to the romance myth, we were suddenly offered its particular coercion, sold as "freedom."[4]

There is a lot at stake in how we relate—the system knows it and always wants to mediate our relationships, isolate us, squander our time, drain our energy, and pit us against each other. Working to resist its pressure to conform connects us to generations of rebels who have fought to dismantle nuclear-family norms and build revolutionary ways for people to be together.

* What parts of the romance myth feel familiar to you? Are there parts that have a hold on you? Can you think of any times when the romance myth has gotten in the way of your relationships? How?
* Are there any points in the section on the Truth About Love that are jarring to read? Are there any that are a relief?
* Have you ever seen yourself act out of character or out of line with your values when under the influence of the romance myth? What would you do differently now?

How the Romance Myth Infects Relationship Self-Help Tools

Dating and relationship self-help tools, ostensibly designed to help bring more insight, often collude with the romance myth's overvaluation of traditional romantic partnerships and undervaluation of other kinds of relationships.

Self-help tools also frequently argue that romantic relationships are *naturally* the most important. Dr. Sue Johnson, author of *Hold Me Tight*, a popular book about attachment styles, writes, "love is . . . the pinnacle of evolution, the most compelling survival mechanism of the human species . . . because [it] drives us to bond emotionally with a precious few others who offer us safe haven."[5] Our current conditions of isolation—in which many people have zero or few close relationships—are the result of social conditions created by racial capitalism and colonialism. Chalking it up to human evolution, rather than social control, is both inaccurate and misleading.

As many do, Johnson cites problematic statistics about how married people live longer.[6] Emotional isolation *is* a health risk, but the claim that *marital* relationships are therefore the healthiest, most evolved ways to organize our lives begs for scrutiny. How does that square, for instance, with the reality of endemic domestic violence?

There's real danger in the assertion that we are biologically "wired" toward particular kinds of relationships and that those relationships are therefore superior. In Johnson's work, as in many relationship self-help books, this includes a harmful claim that committed relationships are always superior to casual sex.

Scarcity Mentality

FROM CHILDHOOD ON, we are taught to compete against the very people we most long to be connected with for the best grades, jobs, dates, etc. We live in a mindset of "compare and despair," always trying to figure out if we are better or worse than others. We are told that if we mess up and fall to the bottom of the hierarchies, we could end up homeless on the streets, abandoned, or dead. We are trained to always look up the hierarchy at what others have that we don't have, and to ignore the experiences of people who have less than us. We are motivated by fear and the idea of scarcity in most realms of life, even when we are not facing real scarcity.

Scarcity mentality doesn't seem like an illusion when we are under its influence. It seems like it's real—that there really isn't enough for everyone, that we have to compete. Cultural norms are like that; they masquerade as truths. Scarcity mentality blocks our creativity and generosity. It makes us distrustful and, sometimes, untrustworthy. We feel like we never have enough time, love, money, or power. It tells us we will soon be too old to find a date, or that we need to "level up" our body, friends, job, house, or car. In reality, none of these things—getting more attention, property, or status—will make us happy.

Psychological researchers who study happiness talk about the difference between being driven by *intrinsic* or *extrinsic* motives. When you are motivated by what is intrinsic, you are doing things because you value them. When you are motivated by what is extrinsic, it is about getting something from the outside: good grades, followers, promotions, or validation. Researchers have found that people who achieve their extrinsic or material (i.e., financial or acquisitive) goals are not measurably happier. However, people who achieve their intrinsic goals, like being a more attentive friend, a compassionate parent, or dancing or making art for pleasure, do become significantly happier.

Studies show that the more extrinsically motivated we are, the more depressed and anxious we become[7]—our relationships get shorter, and their quality declines.[8] That is not surprising. If I am judging people mostly by status or wealth, it is unlikely that I will form warm, trusting connections based on mutual support.

The idea that rich people are happier is fed to us constantly, alongside the myth that anyone can become rich if they work hard. In the US, 35 percent of people believe that they will one day be among the top 1 percent of income earners,[9] and 78 percent of Americans think they can get rich if they work hard enough, even though it is clear that wealth is increasingly concentrated; the rich are getting richer and everyone else is getting poorer.[10] A 2022 study found that 44 percent of US adults believe they have the available tools to become billionaires.[11] A 2023 study found that 69 percent of Gen Zers and 54 percent of millennials who don't currently consider themselves wealthy believe they will become wealthy someday.[12]

Laboring under these misperceptions, we exploit each other and the environment, toil at jobs we hate, or spend time trying to get famous on social media. We learn to compete rather than to connect or collaborate. Racial capitalism encourages us to identify with the elite to the point of voting for elite interests (and against our own) because we mistakenly believe we will someday become them. We won't—and fighting *against* the 1 percent is essential for our survival.

Research shows that consuming commercial media by watching television and spending time online makes us more materialistic.[13] People who spend a lot of time thinking about what they want to buy have reduced empathy and generosity, and end up seeing others as objects.[14] Materialism is bad for our relationships and well-being.[15]

Researchers have found that the number of close friends you have is a better predictor of well-being than income, conventional attractiveness, intelligence, or education. Yet we strive and climb at the expense of our relationships. Advertisements cultivate insecurity in us, and we are exposed to 4,000–10,000 ads *per day*.[16] More eighteen-month-olds can recognize the McDonald's logo than know their own last name. On average, by the time a child is thirty-six months old, she already knows a hundred brand logos.[17]

For most of us, this kind of materialism and status-orientation informs our approaches to dating and sex. We reproduce hierarchies of desirability pitched to us by advertisers and replicated endlessly by social media. We become social climbers who think of our dates and ourselves in terms of status rankings that often correlate to wealth, thinness, wellness, whiteness, and gender norms. We turn into shallow, self-hating consumers even in the realms of sex, love, and romance.

The materialistic emphasis on perfection—on competing to look happy, to show off a perfect life—also insists we "think positive" while shaming "bad" feelings. What actually makes people's lives meaningful is having connected relationships, being part of something you care about, helping others, and playing a role in stopping injustice. These tasks require building—or rebuilding—our capacity to feel difficult things deeply: to be pissed and scared together. When we are mired in scarcity mentality, it can be hard to come together to care for each other and fight back.

The reality is that shit is very, very fucked up and intense right now, and we need skills for being with each other in distress, just as much as we need skills for being with each other in delight. Our attempts to live a life that looks good in photos—filled with status objects and coveted experiences—gets in the way of the unglamorous work of creating and inhabiting the relationships we crave. These relationships—not others' perceptions of who we are—will sustain us through hard times.

* How do you experience scarcity mentality?
* Are there ways in which materialism prevents your happiness?
* Are there ways you have already recovered from scarcity thinking?
* When do you take pleasure in intrinsic value?

Disposability Culture

FROM CHILDHOOD, we are told that there are two kinds of people: "good guys" and "bad guys." It sets us up for a lifetime of fearing being labeled "bad" and striving to be considered "good." We are taught early on to hide parts of ourselves in order to be good. Many of these lessons are nonverbal communications, modeled by our caregivers, that indicate the boundaries of acceptability. As children we are immensely vulnerable, and it is a matter of survival to notice what will garner approval, connection, and safety. We also learn from media representations, peers, and from experiences of humiliation (our own or others') for stepping out of line. For example, we might learn to be a "good girl" by tamping down anger or by professing interest in "girly" things. Or we internalize taboos of all sizes—chew with your mouth closed, don't show your body in public, don't cry, don't yell, give your auntie a hug, smile for the camera.

These lessons become ingrained early on and pursue us into adulthood. *Disposability culture* instills in each of us the fear that if we do one thing wrong, we will be cast out. If I say the wrong thing, will I lose my friends? If people knew what I am really like, would I be rejected? We fear giving and receiving feedback. We become defensive. We learn to look for ways to criticize others that emphasize the ways we are superior. We understand, often unconsciously, that by exposing others' flaws, we can win regard and protect our social status.

Yet the result—back-biting, social media dragging, and "piling on"—can hurt people and tear apart groups. In an ideal situation, we would be able to give and receive critical feedback so that we could grow from mistakes and our relationships could improve. But we are shaped by disposability culture, so we remain vigilant, making sure we are never the next to be thrown out. Paradoxically, living in the high-stakes environment that disposability culture creates can cause us to hide our loved ones' harmful behaviors, fearing they will be judged harshly. In romantic relationships in particular, people often don't tell their friends if their date is hurting them, for fear of their friends thinking the date is "bad." Things get more dangerous as isolation builds.

In reality, rigid disposability norms do not match our lives. We all love some family member who has also hurt us or someone else. We all have a wonderful friend who's terrible when they are drunk or is unreliable with money. We know from lived experience that people are complex, and that harmful behavior often comes from trauma, but living in a culture of disposability makes this hard to remember.

Why do we live in a disposability culture? The world we live in was built by making some people less than human. To justify colonialism and slavery, ideologies were created that made whole groups of people exploitable and killable. The United States imprisons more people than any country that has ever existed on Earth. To maintain a social project of exclusion like that, and to convince everyone that it makes sense to put millions of people, mostly indigenous, Black and brown people, in cages and keep them there, requires an ideology of disposability. It requires a narrative in which some of humanity can be subjugated in the name of protecting and cultivating those deemed good, deserving, and normal.

On an individual level, many of us swing between two poles. Sometimes we fear we will be seen as a bad person. Did I say the wrong thing in that meeting? Is everyone going to find out I am a fraud and not qualified to be here? Other times we revel in our righteousness. Rarely do we spend sufficient time in the nuanced middle, in the reality that everyone is learning, making mistakes, taking risks, and trying things. When conflicts bring up heightened feelings, we often enter a pitched good guy/bad guy mode, turning our lovers, friends, family members, and coworkers into caricatures. (If you are finding yourself in good guy/bad guy thinking because of a conflict, you might try using the What Else Is True? worksheet at the end of this section to get more perspective.)

When people hurt each other, we usually default to one of two polar positions: minimization of the harm, or punishment of the harm-doer. Our society minimizes the impact of harmful systems like racism and sexism all the time, telling people to just brush off racial and sexual harassment, to grow a thick skin, to not get angry. We pretend certain kinds of harm are normal or necessary, or aren't harm at all, like when our criminal system claims that strip-searching arrestees isn't a form of sexual violence. On the other hand, some people face enormous punishment—arrest; deportation; imprisonment; losing their kids, jobs, and housing—for breaking a rule or simply being accused of doing so. The pendulum below[18] represents these extremes of punishment and minimization of harm.

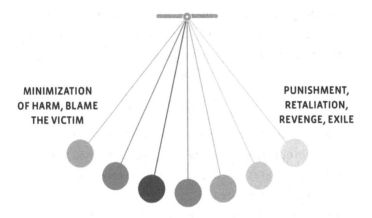

MINIMIZATION OF HARM, BLAME THE VICTIM

PUNISHMENT, RETALIATION, REVENGE, EXILE

When we default to these two extremes, we miss what is in the middle—*accountability.* Accountability is when we assess impact and come up with right-sized responses to it. We acknowledge that someone has been hurt; we think about why that happened, how to prevent it from happening again, and how to attempt repair.

Accountability happens when we look *in a frank and compassionate way* at why harm happened with the aim of making it stop. What does the harm-doer (and maybe others who might do similar harm) need so that they won't do this again? Emotional support; better information about sex, gender, and relationships; support around misuse of alcohol; safe housing? What does the person who was hurt (and people in similar straits) need so that they can be safer? A reliable ride to work, a babysitter on certain nights, a safer place to live, emotional support? Accountability means we look at and address all the conditions that made the harm possible in the first place, rather than denying it even happened or finding a scapegoat for it.

* Can you think of a time when you feared you would be thrown out of a group if you were seen as "the bad guy"?
* Have you ever experienced hurt or harm and other people have minimized it?
* Have you participated in stigmatizing and excluding someone?
* How does being afraid of being "canceled" impact your behavior?
* Can you think of a time when a conflict taught people how to treat each other better and led to stronger bonds?
* What is scary about committing not to throw people away?
* How do you think people should sort out what a right-sized response is to hurt or harm?

"What Else Is True?": Getting Perspective When We're Grabbed by Cultural Scripts and Autopilot Reactions

SOMETIMES WHEN WE get stuck in distorted, binary thoughts and feelings—spiraling about how we are terrible, or someone else is terrible, or that if something specific does or does not happen it's the end of the world—we need to get some perspective. A very simple tool is asking ourselves, "What else is true?" This question can help us find out how our thinking might have gotten narrowed by our own strong reactions. For example, if I am feeling jealous of a partner, and am hyperfocused on the attractive qualities of their new date and my insecurities about our relationship, I can ask, "What else is true?" I could make a list of signs that our relationship is going well. I could make a list of reasons I have chosen non-monogamy. I could make a list of other uncomfortable situations I have survived. I could make a list of reasons I think my partner is not leaving me just because they are connecting with another lover. The What Else Is True? worksheet that follows is useful when you are having strong reactions to sex, romance, and dating experiences. But it is also great for problems at work, with family, in creative collaborations, in activist groups, and with friends. You can fill it out alone, or ask a friend to collaborate with you if you think they might help you see things you can't, in your current state.

What Else Is True? Worksheet

The thing I am feeling strongly: _____

(e.g., Cindy is excluding me from the project and I hate her, or the Network leaves out trans people and the Network is a fucked-up group.)

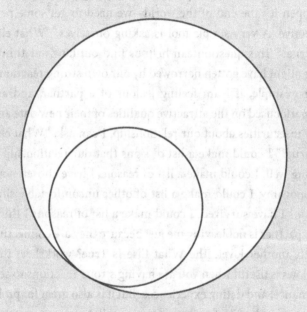

In the small circle, write the thing you are feeling strongly. In the rest of the circle, write about what else is true about this person/group. List positive qualities, benefits, or any other experiences that show a fuller picture. (e.g., "Cindy was a supportive collaborator during the project last year and I saw how thoughtful she was and learned from her." "The Network stood up for active drug users when other organizations wanted to exclude them." "The Network tries hard to live its mission in how it treats employees with kids.")

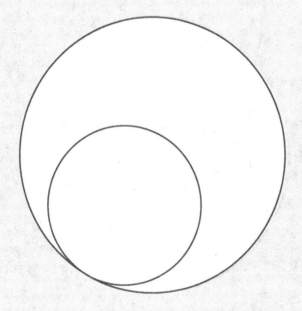

In the small circle, write the thing you are feeling strongly. In the rest of the circle, note "What do I *not* know" that might be contributing to the situation;

what do I *not* know about the other person's/peoples' intentions? (e.g., "Maybe Cindy was not thinking about me when she made that decision." "Maybe Cindy is being impacted by some other personal crisis that is leading to her current actions." "Maybe some people in the Network also disagree with leaving out trans people.")

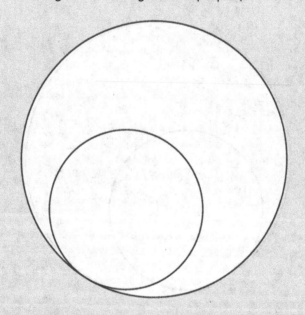

In the small circle, write the thing you are feeling strongly. In the rest of the circle, write what else is true now about your life, beyond this situation? What else do you have going on? Who else do you have as supports? Who stands up for you? Who likes you? (e.g., "I have connected, meaningful collaborations with Lupe and Timothy." "I feel loved and seen by my best friend." "I am excited about the books I am reading right now." "I have friends who agree with me that trans inclusion should never be compromised." "I have years of work ahead of me and behind me that help me see this is just one small moment.")

Fill in the chart below:

What is my responsibility? What can I control or contribute to?	What is beyond my responsibility and control?
....	....
....	....
....	....
....	....
....	....
....	....

Some people might like to rip off the right side of the sheet and throw it away or symbolically give up trying to control it.

Now write down notes about these questions:

* Are there any sore spots from my history this situation might be rubbing against?
* Are there any ways I am in a familiar role in this situation? What feels familiar?
* How can I be kind to myself about those sore spots, or that history, during this period of activation? (Check all those that apply and write in your own below the suggestions.)

    ☐ *Eat a favorite meal from the period in my childhood this reminds me of.*

    ☐ *Take more naps to cope with the stress this is bringing up.*

    ☐ *Ask a friend to listen to me talk about the feelings.*

    ☐ *Go to nature and let myself feel some grief about similar situations in my past.*

    ☐ *Take a bath.*

    ☐ *Go to bed early.*

    ☐ *Take a day off.*

    ☐ *Move my body.*

    ☐ *Write down the feelings that are coming up.*

Why Bother Doing Emotional Work?
What Will This Get Me?

WHEN I FIRST started going to therapy in my early twenties, I feared that if I explored my grief about my mom's illness and death, my life would fall apart. I had suppressed sadness and loneliness from the time my mom got sick when I was twelve. Suppressing these feelings helped me get by while wrestling with school, maneuvering through adolescent social dynamics, taking care of my mom, and then experiencing the shock of her death and moving in with foster parents. But not feeling those emotions had a high cost. Because I had suppressed those memories, I often had a hard time with my memory in general. Because I was suppressing those feelings, I was often insensitive and reactive, not open to emotional awareness more generally. I wasn't very responsible about how my actions and feelings impacted others. I had anxiety and stress patterns—coping mechanisms—that kept the bigger, scarier feelings under wraps. I started therapy because of the discomfort and interpersonal drama that my coping mechanisms were causing, but I was terrified that if I opened up to the grief I had suppressed, I'd fall apart.

It turned out that exploring those feelings did not drown me. Instead, because I had spent such formative years practicing suppressing feelings, rather than being drowned in those feelings, they only gradually became more available.

So now, after decades of emotional work, when I am able to access the grief, loneliness, or anger, to remember missing my mom and what happened, I feel some relief. But I still often find those feelings fleeting and hard to sustain. I share this not because everyone will experience it, but because I wish I had known, when I was so afraid to crack the door on those feelings, that there was little danger of the feelings flooding in and destroying my life and ability to cope. Instead, access to those feelings gives me more access to myself, to connection with others, and to living out my intentions. I am no longer forced to inhabit a tight box of coping that I had to invent as a terrified kid.

We live in a set of systems that want to redirect our desires and deploy them to keep the structures of domination going. We are supposed to limit our marvelous capacities for connection and care to the confines of the romance myth. We are not supposed to find each other, to build deep relationships that transform us, to destroy racial capitalism, and to collectively restore and create liberated ways of being together. The ideas in this book are about changing our relationships to ourselves and to each other so that we can access new kinds of passion, rage, pleasure, and power. When we loosen our conditioning's hold and choose ways of being together that align with our beliefs, we might get to experience:

* Getting out of toxic relationships and dynamics
* Feeling more alive, curious, and creative, thawing out of immobilizing despair and hopelessness
* Increasing our ability to take risks toward what we want, and to tolerate uncertainty
* Creating strong friendships and friendship networks where we feel understood, witnessed, and supported by many people and where we have lots of people's backs
* Enjoying the highs and pleasures of sex, dating, and romance without wrecking our lives about them
* Increasing our ability to trust ourselves and others, to have and feel more safety and security
* Avoiding burnout or recovering from it, so that we know how to collaborate with others in ways that are energizing rather than depleting
* Being able to experience grief, sadness, and anger rather than checking out to avoid those feelings, or suffering from trying to stifle them
* Being able to say no to what we don't want, to make boundaries with people, institutions, and activities in alignment with our values and purpose
* Being able to learn new things, experiment, make mistakes, hear feedback from others, and try again
* Feeling that we belong on Earth and embracing our role in defending the planet and fighting for our own and others' survival

Getting free means deprogramming ourselves, perceiving truths that we are not encouraged to perceive, feeling emotions that we are discouraged from feeling. We are working to recover a broader range of potential responses to the world, beyond programmed reactions. Although I've been taught by society to feel shame and self-hatred in the daily indignities of the workplace or family, I can recover the ability to feel rage, grief, and incitement to action instead. Though I am programmed to try to dominate others, I can choose instead to expand my capacity for collaboration and humility. We can move out of autopilot reactions that have become habitual through repetition, and instead respond to situations and people in ways that are more aligned with our real beliefs and purpose.[19] The point of this healing, then, is to increase our capacities to feel and do new things that make our lives more *on purpose.*[20]

This is different than having a goal of "becoming happy." *Happiness* has a relatively limited, scripted meaning in mainstream capitalist culture and in the popular self-help literature. This imagining of happiness is usually about feeling good all the time, usually because of having achieved normative markers of success such as marriage, wealth, property ownership, and an ideal body type. This goes hand in hand with a belief that any "bad" feelings we have—outrage, fear, grief, confusion, heartbreak—are disorders that need to be treated.

This fantasy of a flat, placated happiness achieved by being rich, skinny, and married is the lifeblood of a consumer culture, and it is totally different from the enlivened, responsive, connective capacity that we actually crave. What we have been told about happiness—that it comes from something extrinsic; that it can be permanently achieved—is likely to make us unhappy. No matter how much money or power people get, they always want more. When people finally get that sought-after status object, they often find it surprisingly disappointing.

Rather than seeking happiness, this book is about trying to wake up to reality, to break free from illusions and conditioned habits. This means we need to let ourselves feel all the fear and grief that living in a world shaped by exploitation, warfare, and ecological devastation generates. It means we must learn to connect with people in ways independent of the romance myth, to see each other more clearly by dispelling the ideas about disposability and scarcity that we have inherited. When we decide to live with each other and ourselves in a way that is based on reality, we can respond to a world in crisis in ways that match our values.

Can People Really Change?

HOW MUCH CAN you actually change by doing the things in a book like this? Medical professionals, pharmaceutical companies, pop psychologists, and pseudoscience sources all tell us that we are hardwired with certain ingrained responses for life. Some people also feel like they can't change because traumatic experiences have fundamentally programmed or limited their range of emotion and behavior.

On the other hand, the world of self-help tells us it can completely transform us in "Just 30 Days!!!" Some people eagerly start new self-transformation programs and methods one after another, each time expecting radical transformation. What's between the poles of total stagnation and total reinvention?

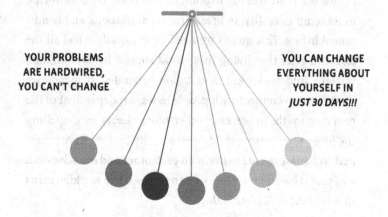

YOUR PROBLEMS ARE HARDWIRED, YOU CAN'T CHANGE

YOU CAN CHANGE EVERYTHING ABOUT YOURSELF IN *JUST 30 DAYS!!!*

The work of *healing*—of knowing what we feel, what we believe in, and of being able to have our actions align with our values—is about a combination of acceptance and transformation, and it is not linear. My own experiences using the tools discussed in this book have led to greater awareness of my autopilot reactions, the limits of my emotional range, the hard or reactive places I go when things get tough.

Sometimes I get frustrated when, despite the level of insight I've gained about my patterns of feeling and relating, I find myself doing the same old shit. We might spend decades trying to change our reactions and behaviors in romantic relationships—reading self-help books, talking with elders, going to therapy—and yet still find old habits creeping up during hard times.

We cannot expect to become totally different people by doing emotional work. We will still have the same wounds we got from the conditions we grew up under, the same familiar coping mechanisms we developed to get by. But by doing this work, we can cut down our reactivity, shorten or minimize periods of emotional activation (aka getting totally freaked out), and begin to learn ways to not act out our harmful impulses. Some people say that healing is a spiral staircase. We may change as we go up, but we will also find ourselves running across our old wounds over and over again as we go around. We do this work so that each time we find ourselves up against the pain of an old pattern, we can at least experience it in a new, more compassionate way, and make new choices about what actions to take in response.

* * *

PERSONAL TRANSFORMATION WORK is similar to changing any habit—it's about shifting autopilot behaviors through intentional practice. Sometimes our old habits creep up, and we're thrown off track. Ideally, we can be caring and compassionate toward ourselves, understanding that transformation is gradual, that we came by our old coping mechanisms honestly and we're not bad for having relied on them, even if we want new ways of living and relating now. With practice, new habits become second nature, available to us most of the time. It is not instantaneous, but change is possible.

Scarcity and disposability thinking causes perfectionism, the idea that someone could or should meet all of society's unrealistic and harmful ideals. Liberation includes letting go of the unrealistic images provided by Hollywood, or organized religion, or by a friend's social media feed. We must remind ourselves and each other: Don't compare your insides to someone else's outsides. We really know very little about what other people are experiencing, and our purpose is to be here in our own lives, looking at what we want to do and how we feel and pursuing transformation that is meaningful to us. Sometimes we can be very hard on ourselves and need to bring more gentleness to that process. Other times we need more rigor and initiative. It can help to ask trustworthy friends if they think you are erring on one side or the other.

Keeping an eye on the dangers of perfectionism and cultivating acceptance is a core part of liberating ourselves from

dominant systems' imperatives. It is no small task to rid ourselves of expectations, reactions, and patterns of relating that
were implanted in us since birth, even if we can see they are
messing up our relationships now. We must approach ourselves with care and compassion, appreciating the lengths
to which we've had to go in order to cope in a competitive,
unkind society where the threat of rejection looms large.
Living under the romance myth, with scarcity mentality, and
in a culture of disposability, is a lot to recover from, and it's
helpful to remember that we are not alone in this. Talking
with our friends and collaborators about our intentions for
how we want to relate and the liberatory principles underlying
them can help us become allies to each other in healing.

- * What about your relational practices are you hoping to
  change?
- * What seem like realistic changes to hope for?
- * How have you effected change in the past?
- * Do your expectations for transformation seem too high
  or too low?
- * What makes it worth being uncomfortable when assessing
  your emotional reactions and your relationships?
- * What do you want more of that you can already imagine
  having? What can you learn from that?

Gentleness and Rigor Assessment Tool

Driven by shame and self-judgment, many of us might think we need more rigor—more dedication, effort, exacting analysis, and hard work—in the very places where we actually need more gentleness. Similarly, if we have been deprioritizing time for rest and relaxation, or for developing our sexuality, for example, we might need to bring more energy and focus to creating more space for those things in our lives. There are also many areas where it is hard for us to change things because of material obstacles, like being stuck at terrible jobs because we have to pay rent. The purpose of this inquiry is to look for where adding either gentleness or rigor could help us move toward what we want where possible, while knowing that there are many conditions in our lives that we do not control.

Consider the following questions in any of these areas of your life:

* Money (e.g., paying bills, spending in ways that align with your values and resources, and being honest with others about money)
* Friendship (e.g., caring for friends, being reliable to friends, and pursuing friendship rather than isolating)
* Health (e.g., taking care of health needs, avoiding things that have difficult health consequences for you, caring

about your body in whatever ways feel kind, and moving
away from internalized ableism or fat shaming)

* Screen time
* Sleep
* Eating, drinking, using substances
* Sex (e.g., following through with actions that will
  enhance your sexual experiences, openly communicating
  with sexual partners, having sex in ways that work for
  you and not in ways that don't, and taking care of sexual
  health)
* Work or schoolwork (e.g., completing things you are
  responsible for, getting out of responsibilities or roles
  that don't work for you if possible, and holding to
  boundaries with others)
* Family
* Activism or organizing
    —What other areas of life would you add to this list?

Where do I need to be more gentle with myself?

* What internal harsh voices do I hear? What do they tell
  me? Do these voices sound like parents, teachers, siblings,
  bosses, or others who have judged me in the past?
* What am I afraid would happen if I were more gentle with
  myself?

In what areas do I need more rigor?

* What gets in the way of my taking steps toward things I believe in or want?
* How could I get support to take those steps?
* What is a reasonable place to start with rigor that is right-sized, not harsh or based in shaming and judging myself?

Some Notes on Self-Help Books about Romantic Relationships (or Marriage, as They Call It)

For all the reasons explored so far, we really need some new ways of thinking about sex, romance, and relationships, so that we can stop acting out our conditioning with each other and tearing apart our friend circles and social movement groups. However, the relationship self-help book genre leaves a lot to be desired. Some of the main problems with this type of literature, which make it unappealing and unlikely to be of maximum use to radicals, are that:

* It is mostly written by, for, and about upper-class, white, straight, Christian people. Many of the books are explicitly racist and are written as if queer and trans people and poor people do not exist or are inferior.

* It mostly presumes that it is better to stay in relationships than to get out of them, and that wanting anything besides a lifelong committed monogamous relationship is a sign of dysfunction, selfishness, or immaturity.
* It presumes that romantic relationships are the primary source for getting emotional needs met, and disregards the importance of friendship. It also ignores the fact that many of the dynamics it describes happen not just in romantic relationships but also in friendships and between coworkers and collaborators in political and creative work.
* It often uses pseudoscientific evidence to assert that the gender binary or the romance myth is natural.
* It pathologizes and stigmatizes neurodiversity.
* It assumes white, patriarchal, colonial, capitalist, ableist norms when evaluating what "good" partners and children and "functional" relationships look like, and gives advice for assimilating into those systems instead of suggesting ways of destroying them.

Despite these drawbacks, there are some useful insights and tools in the standard literature of relationship self-help books, but you have to read between the lines to find the good stuff. For many, the experience might be too enraging or damaging.

Having to read something that disregards who you are or writes you out of existence can be too painful for you to do much healing. For that reason, I am sharing here the tools I have found useful from that literature, and have framed them in the way I wish they had been written. I am hoping that by reinterpreting these ideas through liberating political lenses, such as feminism, anticapitalism, and antiracism, they can be of greater use to people in resistance movements.

You Are What You Practice

THE IDEA OF *PRACTICE* can help us link our day-to-day, moment-to-moment behaviors and feelings to the broader arc of our lives. A practice is anything that you do repeatedly. Doing things over and over again creates a well-worn path. Those things become the easiest to do again. Lots of our practices are unintentional and unconscious, things we aren't really choosing to do, just replaying out of habit. Perhaps when under pressure you zone out, or during conflict you freeze up and can't think, or when scared you lash out. The aim of this liberation work is to practice more things on purpose. When our practices become outdated, they don't match our current beliefs and desires, or they get us into situations that we don't like. To change our practices we have to be intentional about new practices we want to adopt.

These three phrases, which I have encountered from multiple teachers, have been powerful reminders to me:

* You are what you practice, and you are always practicing something.
* How you do anything is how you do everything.
* What you pay attention to grows.[21]

We can inquire: What am I practicing again and again so that it is almost automatic? What practices could I introduce that would move me toward what I want to do and feel?

An example is how we relate to our screens. In the age of smartphones, most people have adopted the practices corporations intend us to perform: we pick our phones up frequently, we interrupt our conversations and tasks to check them. This distracts our minds and shortens our attention spans. Many people report having a harder time reading, writing, or focusing on any one task for long because of the practice of being interrupted frequently. Fifty-seven percent of Americans do not read a single book in a typical year. Instead, they spend an average 5.4 hours on their phone each day.[22] Many don't even notice when they pick up their phones, or wander off into social media while trying to complete a more involved task. Repeated practice leads to automatic behavior, something that ends up feeling involuntary or unconscious.

Psychology researchers tell us that habits form through repetition and create neural pathways in our brains, so that we become wired to continue to repeat the behavior. Habits operate through a *cue*, *routine*, and *reward* cycle.[23] We get the cue, such as seeing the phone light up with a notification, or feeling bored, or being cranky about the task we're doing; we unconsciously crave some distraction. Then we follow the routine and reach for the phone, opening whatever series of apps we have created a habitual practice of checking. Then we feel the reward. That reward doesn't have to be something good, like seeing a wonderful message from a friend or getting a hot picture from a date. Just opening apps, or finding anything at all, or even hearing the ding of a notification, is enough to trigger a reward feeling in our brains.[24]

Investigating how we have been or are rewarded by our habitual practices, even if the reward doesn't feel that good, can help us build more awareness around these practices. Similarly, noticing which initial cues trigger our habitual practices can be helpful—one example might be that looking in a mirror could generate hypercritical thinking about your body. If we know the cue, we may be able to intervene when the routine is about to start.

You may have a habitual practice of rushing. Many people eat very quickly, because they formed a habit of rushing to eat before school or work, and now end up eating quickly even when there is more time available. Perhaps you walk or drive quickly and impatiently, even when there is nothing to rush toward and even though it creates a feeling of stress. Perhaps you have a practice of looking at others critically, something you learned from your family or from popular media: you feel inclined to criticize others' bodies or clothing. Or maybe you are well-practiced at looking at your own body and appearance and saying unkind things to yourself in your head. You may not even consider these things practices, because the thoughts pop into your head without effort. Our practices determine so much of what we feel and think, what seems possible to us, and how we connect with others.

Organizations, social groups, and families also have practices and group norms about feelings that are often unconscious, like rushing, over-promising and under-delivering, being cliquish, being disorganized, not listening carefully, being checked out, or being hierarchical. Looking at how we practice certain behaviors, thoughts and feelings over and over, by ourselves or as part of groups, can offer us a way of approaching changes we want to make in a very practical, next-small-step way.

Many of us practice what was practiced in our families. Most of us took up limited roles to survive in those groups. Maybe you are the caregiver in the family, or the anxious one, or the one who always needs help, or the person who hides and is quiet. We sometimes find ourselves taking on these roles again in friendships, in romantic relationships, at work, or in activism. Some of our family practices might be ones that serve us and that we want to retain, but others might be ones we want to move away from. This is one of the reasons that visiting family can be so difficult—we might find ourselves thrust back into practices that we've outgrown in the rest of our lives, ones that feel particularly ill-fitting now.

Many of us practice certain behaviors and feelings with romantic or sexual partners that we do not do with other friends, like being more jealous, controlling, helpless, fearful, stingy, passive, punitive, or resentful. Sometimes this means we feel like our "worst selves" with these people. Because romantic and sexual relationships often activate our core insecurities and wounds that originate from childhood, some of our hardest feelings and most regrettable behaviors can show up in our romantic and sexual relationships. This also means that these relationships can be special places for examining well-worn practices and finding pathways to having more choice about what we are doing.

We can understand our daily lives as a collection of practiced behaviors, thoughts, and feelings. My friend Craig once told me that he thinks of his brain as having well-worn channels, like the grooves in a vinyl record album. Emotions he has felt again and again come to the surface more readily than others. And I think this is can be said of most of us. These grooves are patterns that we fall into more easily because of how deeply they've been carved into us.

For some of us, anxiety will leap up to the surface first. For others, it will be anger or fear. Some of us have spent so much time feeling different, alone, or out of place in groups that we find the experience of alienation emerging automatically, even when we finally join a group or attend a gathering with more people like us. We might notice ourselves looking for evidence that we are outsiders, misunderstood, or unappreciated—our brain is searching for reasons to feel that way, interpreting everything through that lens. We have insufficient practice with *belonging*, so we have a hard time feeling it, even if we long for it and an opportunity presents itself. Some of us have spent so much time giving care and attention to others that we have a hard time receiving it ourselves. Some of us have practiced being tough or being numb for so long that we struggle to allow ourselves to be vulnerable.

We could even see our own identities as a set of repeated feelings, beliefs, and behaviors—something feminist philosopher Judith Butler famously wrote about in the 1990s. Butler argued that our genders are collections of repeat performances, rather than stable or natural ways of being.[25] Seeing our identities this way, as something that we practice—and as something that might change as we practice differently in different spaces or at different points in our lives—is a radical departure from cultural myths about gender. These myths hold that people are born into strict identity categories and will "naturally" follow the rules of those categories unless there is something "wrong" with us.

This critical idea—that identities are a result of repeated practice rather than natural categories—invites us to approach our own conceptions of ourselves differently, less rigidly. Our identities often feel fixed, because we are forcibly scripted into them by the dominant culture. Other people punish and reward us for failing or succeeding to behave according to norms. And we become attached to our various identities as places where we can feel belonging, solidarity, affirmation, and connection. There is nothing wrong with that, and in fact, resistance and solidarity often include proudly asserting stigmatized or countercultural identities.

But what happens with the perspective that our identities—whether political ones like identifying with a race or gender or sexual identity, or other, disposition- or role-based identities, like seeing ourselves as a leader, an angry person, the truth-teller in any group, the person who always gets left out—are a result of practices, even if they are habituated, well-worn practices? How might our lives and relationships to each other change if we thought we could bring curiosity and intention to areas that seem hard-wired? To parts of ourselves that we've been told are fixed and stable, or to roles we are attached to or feel stuck in?

The idea that we are what we practice can be liberating. Yes, it is difficult to change a practice. But it is wonderful to imagine that we are not permanently, passively "stuck," "damaged," or "broken." We can experiment with new practices. If we at least *sometimes* get to have a different experience, or we notice that a moment is a result of practice rather than being fixed and predetermined, we will be freer.

This work of noticing unconscious practices is a core component to the social transformation that we long for when we fight racism, sexism, and ableism. We might notice that we have been socialized to feel inferior and not share our ideas, so we explore methods of speaking up and feeling our dignity. We might notice that we have been socialized to feel superior and to take up space, so we can begin, say, to practice listening carefully and waiting to assert ourselves in meetings or classes.

We might have been socialized to expect others to clean up after us, so we learn to notice if we are making messes or not participating in cleanup. We strive to notice patterns of practice and their impacts on ourselves and others. And we sometimes develop shared new practices. An example of this is how, in many group spaces these days, we share our names, pronouns, and access needs at the beginning. This has become second nature within many groups as a practical solution to significant obstacles to participation. The first time, a new practice such as this might seem novel or odd, but after just a few repetitions, it becomes ordinary.

Analyzing our behaviors and feeling states by asking "What am I practicing?" can support a sense that it is possible to choose new ways of behaving, thinking and feeling over time. We can also make this inquiry within relationships—"What are *we* practicing together?" A couple might notice that their relationship is isolating them, and make shared efforts to change it. Or two friends might realize that they always focus on one person's stories and experiences, and might decide to shift that attention, together. People in friendships or dating relationships can also choose practices they want to add to their lives that will be easier to do with a collaborator, like reading together, or going to see art together, or learning to cook or dance together, or meditating together.

Changing what we practice is not easy. The more we have repeated something, the easier it is to keep doing it and not even notice that we're doing so. If, for years on end, every time you see your reflection you negatively assess your appearance, changing that won't happen overnight. If, for years, you routinely procrastinate doing important tasks, it is hard to stop on a dime.

Often we have very compelling reasons for having developed practices, even self-defeating ones, because they were originally created to protect us from harm. Many people struggle with anxiety because they grew up in stressful conditions where fretting over doing things right—whether to avoid a parent's anger, or to make sure they got by at school, or to make sure the bills were paid—was essential to survival. Now, even if they are in a relatively safe situation, they can't stop anxious thoughts from intruding. These are well-worn patterns of thinking and feeling, and we have to be compassionate with ourselves as we become more aware of them repeating in our lives.

The practice framework, while not suggesting that transformation is easy, does invite the idea that we can move toward lives that align more and more with our values and desires. Many of the activities in this book offer ways to notice what we are practicing on autopilot, especially when we are enacting cultural scripts that do not serve our liberation or increase our connection to each other. Ultimately, the goal is to choose new, more deliberate practices that will lead to our shared flourishing.

Chapter One Recap

* We're living in hard times and we really need each other, but we often treat each other poorly and lose connection.
* Crappy cultural scripts shape our expectations about relationships and make us think that those scripts are our authentic feelings and desires.
* Childhood pressures, limits, and judgments (from families, schools, jobs, faith communities, etc.) force us to adapt coping behaviors that can later become unhelpful in our relationships.

* Many of our thoughts, feelings, and behaviors are habitual practices that we aren't conscious of or think are fixed parts of our personality. Investigating them can allow us to more actively decide how to live, relate with others, and feel.

* Uncovering and breaking harmful, system-serving illusions and patterns of behavior allows us to pursue what we really believe in and desire.

Stuck on Autopilot: Swinging between Numbness and Temporary Highs

Under empire, happiness is seen as a duty . . . Empire . . . works to keep its subjects stuck in individualizing sadness: held in habits and relationships that are depleting, toxic, and privatized. This stagnation might be held in place by the pursuit of happiness, and the attempt to numb or avoid pain. To be more fully present, in contrast, means tuning in to that which affects us, and participating actively in the forces that shape us.

—CARLA BERGMAN AND NICK MONTGOMERY,
Joyful Militancy: Building Thriving Resistance in Toxic Times

YOUR HEART IS A MUSCLE THE SIZE OF YOUR FIST.
KEEP LOVING. KEEP FIGHTING.
—DALIA SAPON-SHEVIN, from a print made for the 1999 WTO Protests in Seattle

SOME PEOPLE WORRY that they have too many feelings that are too strong, that they are too sensitive. Others feel like they are too insensitive, too impatient with other people's feelings, or that they are a bit dead inside. This chapter looks at how dominant culture shapes us to be simultaneously numb (especially to our own pain and others') and in perpetual pursuit of fantasies about feeling amazing that are tied to consumerism and meeting social norms. In the face of these pressures, we can dedicate ourselves to liberating our feelings—to escaping from harmful scripts that have told us what to feel and not feel. Doing so is an act of resistance that makes us better able to respond to the conditions we're facing—to percieve reality and take action. For most of us, this means feeling *more* than we've been told to feel, reclaiming our emotional range.

This chapter begins by focusing on the pressure to be numb. This is essential in a society that causes us to live with so much loss and suffering. This is why the psychiatric profession has made grief a diagnosable disorder. Over the years, *The Diagnostic and Statistical Manual of Mental Disorders* (DSM)—the reference book used by mental health professionals to diagnose—has increasingly pathologized grief. At one time, the DSM had a "grief exception" to diagnoses of depression. If a person was reporting symptoms of depression but had had a significant loss in the past year, they were understood to be grieving rather than to have a "disorder." However, that window was later shrunk to three months, and then to two weeks.[1] Apparently, if you feel bad more than two weeks after your loved one dies, the psychiatric profession labels your brain "disordered."

We are living under conditions of ecological crisis, war, police and border violence, mass shootings, ongoing genocides, housing and food insecurity around the world and in our immediate communities—it is offensive to be told that grief is a disorder. How could we not be grieving and aggrieved? Yet jobs, doctors, and cultural institutions tell us that grief is inappropriate or taboo.

In this context, choosing to experience grief, sorrow, and other stigmatized feelings is, as psychotherapist Francis Weller puts it, rebellious. To feel these things is to "resist the demands to remain passive and still."[2] As we increase our capacity to feel, we also become better able to care for others' strong feelings, making us a source of support for our embattled communities.[3]

Next, we'll look at how teaching us to be numb to our own and others' pain creates a dynamic of either minimizing hurt or seeking vengeance. In disposability culture, we don't get to have right-sized experiences of being hurt or finding out we are causing others pain, and instead we oscillate between denying that bad things happen and creating a scapegoat to punish.

Finally, we'll dive into how, in a society where we are supposed to mostly numb out to get by, we can get fixated on chasing fantastical feelings, especially in the realm of sex and romance. We are compelled by the fantasy of finding total happiness or thrilling excitement through sex and romance.

Many of us seek biochemical highs from flirting, sex apps, porn, escalating relationships, obsessing over exes, crushing, and the like. But a romantic or sexual life built on chasing highs and romance-myth illusions can lead to all kinds of difficulty. This section explores what we might do to find alternative ways to enjoy these activities and connections, ways not driven by romance-myth escapist fantasies.

Numbing to Get By in a Painful World

Nova is bored by school and doesn't have a lot of friends. She feels awkward around most people. She really only feels good when she is researching workout routines by looking at fitness influencers on Instagram, or after she does a really hard workout. There's nothing better than the sweaty exhaustion and feeling of accomplishment. If she could look like the people she follows on social media, life would get better, and she could finally relax and feel okay.

Zafir is constantly anxious about the state of the world, especially climate change. He finds himself doomscrolling a lot and, to release some of the tension, he often logs in to his favorite video game and plays for hours. It's like there are only two states of being for him: filled with adrenaline and excitement in the video game; or worried and immobilized, staring at his phone.

Ash has recently shifted a lot of their attention away from both playing soccer with friends and the needle exchange project they used to work on. After starting hormones a year ago, they set up profiles on some sex apps, where they can message and flirt, looking for hookups. The excitement of meeting strangers, and the possibility that something really wild or hot might happen, makes them obsessively check the apps and spend hours trying to arrange dates. A lot of it ends up being kind of boring or disappointing, but when someone is hot for their trans body, they feel desirable, and eager to connect.*

The systems we live under want us numb to certain feelings—numb enough to toil at boring jobs, to experience or witness or participate in injustices without resisting. At the same time they manipulate our desires for joy, stimulation, and connection, keeping us in search of mythical peak experiences like getting rich and famous, looking flawless, or finding the perfect sex or romance. To get by in our families and school and a punishing society, we close down our full range of feelings. Many of us have a hard time even knowing what we feel, or taking our emotions (or others') seriously. As Francis Weller has observed, we have a culture of "amnesia and anesthesia—we forget, and we go numb."[4]

---

* These vignettes are composites of common stories and dynamics.
Any identifying information about individuals has been removed.

For those of us who long for justice, this rings deeply familiar. Dominant systems pretend that there are no power imbalances, that current arrangements are fair and neutral, and that we should all just be out for ourselves, trying to get ahead. For example, we see how men are consistently trained not to have empathy for people experiencing sexual violence. Men are taught to participate in cultural rituals that tolerate or celebrate violence against women and queers. White people are conditioned to discount accounts of racism, large and small, and to consistently dehumanize people of color. Numbness, distraction, and forgetting are essential methods of control, for many reasons:

* It is painful to see other people suffering, so we desensitize.

* It hurts to be faced with evidence that the systems we live under are not fair, that illegitimate authorities protect some and attack others. Headlines and social media bombard us with heartbreaking news about loss of life, injustice, and destruction. We build barriers to feeling this pain.

* The systems work best if we have limited empathy. They need us to take up roles dominating or extracting from others or benefitting from others' subjection.

* The systems want us to be numb to the pain that comes from being targeted and exploited, to have a "thick skin" and not resist. We learn that, to get by, we need to feel as little as possible.

Mostly Numb, but Chasing Fantasies

WE BECOME WELL practiced at numbing in order to survive. After shaping us into people with smaller ranges of emotion and less access to empathy, these same systems then sell us back promises of feeling fantastic—quick and easy euphoria and escape from the boredom of being numb. We want to feel alive.

We see representations of other people's lives that suggest they feel amazing, and romantic movies, songs, and books that tell us that love is about feeling like you would die for someone, like you will die without them, and that you would give anything and everything for them. Sex is supposed to be mind-blowing, and hanging out with friends needs to be the party of a lifetime, resulting in glamorous photos and hilarious stories. We watch action movies, play video games, and consume substances seeking highs and escape. *We want to feel*, but we have a hard time feeling (after so much practice numbing) without the help of consumer experiences or distorted cultural fantasies.

Our ability to feel is intimately bound up with the very systems that numb us. Chasing consumer highs and adrenaline thrills can operate as anesthesia, rather than help us connect to authentic feelings of aliveness. We are told we can be happy when we are going to Disneyland, or when someone finally buys us a diamond, or when we win at the casino. Cecile Andrews, an author and community educator whose work focuses on why and how people might reject consumerism and choose to live more simply, argues that to control us through consumerism, the owning class wants us both numb and chasing limited kinds of excitement:

> When we no longer know what we feel, we're open to being manipulated by Fast culture: advertising, marketing, consumerism, status, power. In our emptiness, we adopt the responses they want us to feel. The manipulators are able to make us get excited about all sorts of things, like a pair of jeans or a diamond ring or a get-rich-quick candidate.[5]

Francis Weller, whose work focuses on grief, argues that we live "shallow lives, pocked by meaningless routines and the secondary satisfaction of happy hour" because we are captured by a societal mandate of productivity and a fiction of material gain. He argues that we deserve to be more alive than this, that "[w]e are the inheritors of an amazing lineage, rippling with memories of life lived intimately with bison and gazelle, raven and the night sky. . . designed to encounter this life with amazement and wonder, not resignation and endurance."[6] We need to experience grief and sorrow to feel fully alive.

He observes that there is "some strange intimacy between grief and aliveness, some sacred exchange between what seems unbearable and what is most exquisitely alive."[7] Because the systems we live under need us numb, "[e]ntire industries have emerged to keep the senses dulled and distracted. Our need to be anesthetized is rooted in our smoldering dissatisfaction with the meager existence we have been offered by this society."[8]

Numbness, anxiety, depression, isolation, boredom, and disconnection are the norm, and we are taught to chase experiences and products marketed as providing relief from the pain of our lives. So much of what we feel compulsive about—obsessing over a crush, checking dating apps, playing video games, consuming substances, shopping—are part of this pattern of both numbing out and trying to feel alive. Nowhere is this dynamic more obvious than on social media. We portray ourselves in ways we hope will get us approval or attention online, then wait obsessively for the hit of oxytocin that comes when others share and like the content we post. The emergence of social media has increased the fantasy of being individually famous. The problem of focusing on extrinsic satisfaction is heightened when we are encouraged to chase ever more outlandish kinds of approval.

Given that we are told to think about our lives through consumerist fantasies, it is not surprising that when we desire healing, we are vulnerable to overblown promises. We are trained to want healing that is fast, miraculous, and extreme. Self-help regimes of all kinds promise to make you skinny, rich, happy, loved, and famous—in just those thirty days.

In real life, healing is a lifelong journey, requiring us to experiment with feeling, resist the pressure to be numb, and face fears as we try new practices. It also necessitates learning to accept that many things about us will not change, or will not change dramatically. Given this context, cultivating the ability to notice and feel subtle things is powerful, transformative, and rebellious.

Building Awareness of Nuance and Subtlety

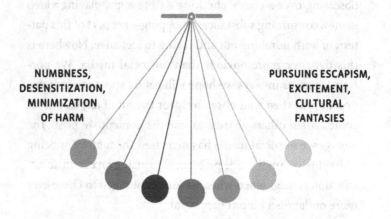

NUMBNESS, DESENSITIZATION, MINIMIZATION OF HARM

PURSUING ESCAPISM, EXCITEMENT, CULTURAL FANTASIES

Under current conditions we are asked to live through these two polar experiences. We numb ourselves to others' pain and the pain of benefiting from unfair hierarchies. We become numb to our own pain when we're being targeted or exploited, trying to have a "thick skin." This helps us survive while we're forced to witness and experience constant injustice.

At the same time, we chase the fantasies offered by consumer culture—having the perfect body, the best clothes, the car, vacation, relationship. We're taught to believe these things will finally make us happy and relieve the boredom of numbing out. We try to feel alive by getting thrills from video games, violent movies, substances, chasing sexual or romantic fantasies, and other escapes.

Learning to notice the subtleties we have been taught to ignore could seem unrewarding. Would becoming more aware of other people's feelings and experiences mean that we have to take more responsibility for our impact on them or act toward them with greater care? Would it leave less time to strive for the fantastical rewards as we attend to the actual sensations of our lives? Some of those sensations might seem boring compared to the promise of extremes that motivate our compulsions. I have often heard people who were getting sober from some kind of addiction talk about how, at first, they feared life would be boring if they gave up the behavior or substance, even though they had reached a point where they saw it messing up their life. What would it be like to go through the world not seeking their high, they wondered? That fear of the boringness of ordinary real life is legitimate.

So much of the work people are doing for justice and liberation is about exposing reality and working to transform harmful distortions. Corporations want us glued to our phones, not paying attention to the stories of our elders and children, the change of seasons, the migration of birds. To become connected to each other and responsive to conditions, we need to break out of patterns of feeling and not-feeling that were set by a culture that wants us numb and addicted. We need to become the sensing, feeling animals we were born to be.

Recovering Our Full Emotional Range

Part of being numb, chasing highs, and losing access to subtle feelings is having a limited set of feelings we default to, like we're playing cards but don't have the full deck. Accessing more emotions means experiencing more of life. Some of us grew up in situations where interactions with adults were unsafe and unpredictable; we may have become anxious and vigilant, trying to please adults and reduce their explosions or reactivity, keep connections to meet our basic needs. We got good at feelings like caution, gratitude, shame, and anxiety, and turned off anger, sadness, and grief. Other people handled their childhood circumstances by being tough and bold, relying on anger, stoicism, and recklessness, and turning off fear, sadness, and appreciation. Some people got by being "cheerful" and entertaining, and now have trouble accessing emotions they were told were "negative" by their caregivers. Everyone has certain feelings that come easily and others that are rarely felt. All of us can gain more connection to others and increase our sense of security and well-being as we explore these limitations and build more capacity to feel the full spectrum of emotion.

* What feelings come most easily to you?
* Which are taboo or inaccessible?
* Are there feelings you hear other people talk about that you have never felt?
* Are there feelings to which you want more access?
* Do you get stuck in certain feelings that you want to shake loose from? (See p. 211 for a list of feelings in case that helps.)

Tools for Building Emotional Awareness

HERE ARE SOME broad categories of tools and practices that can enhance awareness of our emotions and can expand our emotional range:

* **Meditation:** Meditation helps us observe patterns of thinking, feeling, and reacting. It can help us get some critical distance from autopilot responses and allow us to make more choices.

* **Bodywork and Body Movement:** The pressure to be numb includes being oblivious to the sensations of our bodies. In order to survive the systems of social control we live in, we ignore many of our bodies' sensations and needs. Finding bodywork methods to explore—on our own or with a practitioner—can increase our awareness of bodily sensations and help us investigate feelings of pain, shame, trauma, pleasure, and healing.

* **Talk Therapy:** Talk therapy can provide a space for reflecting on our feelings and the experiences that have shaped and perhaps restricted our emotional range.

* **12-Step Programs:** These provide free meeting spaces (both online and in person) where we can listen to other people talk about their feelings and experiences with alcohol, drugs, internet use, sex/romance, work, food, relationships with people in crisis, and more, and where we can share ours if we want.

* **Journaling:** Writing down how we are feeling can help us pay more attention to what thoughts and emotions

are emerging and how they might connect to early formative experiences.

* **Finding Out about Feelings:** For some of us, feelings seem like a mystery. But it is important to investigate them. We can read about feelings in fiction, memoir, or self-help books; listen to psychology podcasts; or listen to friends describe their feelings in order to find out how other people feel and to look for those sensations in ourselves, or to notice what we don't relate to about others' feelings. Other kinds of media can also sometimes stir feelings. We can watch sad movies to practice crying, or nature documentaries to observe nurturance between adults and young.

* **Connecting to Nature:** The immensity of the ocean, mountains, or sky; the passage of seasons; and cycles of growth, death, decay, and rebirth, all can help us re-enter ourselves and access reflection and subtle sensations.

* **Art Practice:** Capitalism asks most of us to turn off our creativity early in life. If we are not picked out as the artist at school, we tell ourselves we are bad at art, singing, dancing, or whatever the creative pursuit, and stop trying. We are only supposed to pursue creativity if we can compete in the corporate market. Exploring creativity and expression can feel taboo and even shameful, but if we can find a way into art practice, we experience ourselves differently.

Costs of a Limited Emotional Range

EMOTIONAL AWARENESS IS worth pursuing, in order for us to get better at relating to people and fighting for survival and liberation. When we lack connection to our own feelings, we may:

* Have a hard time being around others when they are having strong feelings. We might give unsolicited advice because we want others to feel better fast, or might actively minimize what they are experiencing.

* Get overwhelmed by strong feelings when we do have them, losing sight of how to act within our values.

* Go along too much with someone else's strong feelings, piling on or joining, even if it's reactive or justifies bad behavior.

* Get defensive or fall into a shame spiral if someone else's strong feelings are about us, rather than listening and working to discern what we think is true.

* Become conflict-avoidant, sidestepping direct feedback in favor of secret lists of resentments and gossip, or ghosting on important relationships if the other person brings up issues that scare us.

* Lie or hide things to avoid our own feelings or the fallout of stirring up someone else's.

Even as we long for intimacy and connection, numbness makes them hard to sustain. It becomes worth it, however, to risk feeling more when we finally tire of cycles of drama, of losing friends or lovers, of finding ourselves frustrated with repeating patterns. Pursuing subtlety is, in fact, radical and rebellious and central to living in reality so we can fight for liberation. If we can't feel, we can't truly assess what is currently happening, care for each other, make decisions together, live our values, and be accountable to ourselves and each other. De-numbing and attuning to subtlety are lifelong practices. It is not merely that this is similar to dismantling internalized systems of domination. It is *because* dismantling those systems inside and outside ourselves requires being able to feel more.

Numbness and Emotional Labor

FEMINISTS REMIND US that women, and especially women of color, often do extensive, unappreciated, uncompensated emotional labor in relationships, families, and organizations. Emotional labor is the work people do to maintain relationships, give others emotional support, and keep groups together by attending to people's feelings. Because feeling is not valued in dominant society, but people still have feelings, the work of noticing how people are doing, addressing social dynamics, and coping with crises is unpaid, unrecognized work.

Women are expected to be sensitive and do this work, and face stigma and exclusion if they do not, while insensitivity is tolerated (and sometimes valued) in men, and white people in general. We can shift this unfair imbalance by valuing and building sensitivity, emotional awareness, and emotional connection in individuals and groups. We heal by noticing where we have been made numb and learning to bring attention there, and also by noticing who gets to be numb and who has to be hypervigilant and attentive to others' feelings to keep things going. Dominant systems assign these roles through gender, race, and other hierarchies.

Numbness and Respectability Politics

COMPULSORY NUMBNESS, SCARCITY, and materialism also relate to contemporary criticism of *respectability politics*: a political strategy that says that people who want to fight for justice should look and act in ways that meet mainstream norms of professionalism or reasonableness. It says that resistance groups should be run like businesses and have leaders who act like bosses.

We are encouraged to compete with each other for grants from rich people, for media attention, and for jobs in nonprofits where we are pressured to shape our work toward the whims of philanthropists. Elites reward us for narrowing our message, reducing our demands, and leaving out stigmatized and vulnerable people. We are told that if we want to make change, we need to "get a place at the table." But getting to those tables requires us to shape ourselves around all the norms and structures we should be tearing down, to mimic the race and gender norms that read as "professional," to speak languages of appeasement to power as if those in control will change their minds about domination if we are just polite and reasonable enough. Aware of the traps and pitfalls of respectability politics in the past, resistance movements now relentlessly work to revive and sustain other ways of fighting back—our ways. We cultivate horizontal structures centered in transparency, so that our groups belong to the people involved in and impacted by their work—that's who should be making decisions. And we are suspicious of accepting money from our opponents (corporations, philanthropists, governments), of appealing to their institutions for change or trying to change them from the inside. We know, and have known for a long time, that these "legitimate" and rewarded paths are set up to make us ineffective.

Building horizontal, transparent, transformative collaborations is challenging to put into practice, though. No matter how radical our thinking, we have still been shaped by systems that trained us to be numb, unsatisfied, status-oriented, and competitive—characteristics that foster disconnectivity from one another. We have to intentionally put into practice new kinds of emotional awareness and build new skills in order to create the kind of movement culture, relationships, and groups we crave and need.

Numbness and Microaggressions

MICROAGGRESSIONS IS A TERM antiracists use for describing the constant subtle, sometimes unintentional acts against people with targeted identities that happen at work, at school, in families, all the time. It might be hearing small comments, being left out, being stared at, or being asked the same question over and over, like "Where are you from?" or "How do you have sex?" or "Can I touch your hair?" Living in an environment where people repeatedly, usually unconsciously, reinforce cultural scripts that exclude, marginalize, and belittle others has big cumulative impacts on our lives.

Microaggressions are relentless, and their significance is minimized by perpetrators and witnesses. People are told they should have a thick skin, are "too sensitive" or "too angry," if they complain. People harmed by microaggressions should be allowed to feel the harm and complain about it, and people doing the harm need to de-numb and become aware of and responsible for the impact their actions have.

When someone tells us we hurt them, we are trained to deny, to argue "I didn't mean it that way." We are not just trained to say this, we are trained to feel it—to be numb to the harm we cause, unaware of power dynamics when we are in the dominant position. Our fear of being labeled "the racist" or "the sexist" or "the bad guy" makes us afraid to find out how we hurt others. To build a new world based on connected relationships, we have to open up to increased sensation—including grief and anger that these power differentials exist—alongside the discomfort of acknowledging when we are on the dominant side of some of them, unconsciously yet harmfully acting out their scripts. If we want liberation, we must be actively curious and root out cultural programming and autopilot numbness that keep us unintentionally enforcing those hierarchies.

Numbness and Chasing Fantasies Questionnaire

How do you numb out? Check all that apply and write in others. Note that all of these are activities that can be good parts of our lives—there is nothing inherently wrong with them—it's just a question of whether we are using them to numb ourselves and how we might want to take action once we are aware of that.

☐ *Online shopping*   ☐ *Gossip*

☐ *Dating apps*   ☐ *Video games*

☐ *Social media*   ☐ *Reading*

☐ *TV*   ☐ *Exercise*

☐ *Porn*   ☐ *Cleaning*

☐ *Sleep*   —What else?

How can you tell which are pleasurable, relaxing activities that build resilience and which are numbing out? When you turn to these activities, ask yourself:

* What kinds of feelings or moments brought you here? (e.g., procrastinating, receiving bad news, worrying about something, escapism)
* How do you feel during, and after? (e.g., more relaxed, connected, alive, numb, restless, tired, or blank)
* Did you intend to do this, or had you told yourself you would not? Does it disrupt something, like getting enough sleep, connecting with other people, or completing tasks that are important to you?

Living with a lot of numbing, many of us chase feelings of aliveness in ways that are often unsatisfying. We chase things that we have been told will make us permanently happy (in truth, nothing creates permanent happiness). Do you find yourself chasing anything in a way that is imbalanced, or based on cultural ideals you know to be untrue?

☐ *A certain body type*
☐ *More money*
☐ *Cool friends*

☐ *The best party*
☐ *The perfect home*
☐ *Hot sex*
☐ *The right partner*

☐ *The perfect creation*
  (writing, music,
  visual art, etc.)

☐ *The perfect job*

☐ *Perfect health and/or*
  fitness

☐ *The right clothes*

☐ *The right car*

☐ *The best vacation*

—What else?

Then ask yourself:

* Where did you get the idea of what are the right or perfect
  versions of these things?

* Can you imagine being satisfied in these areas of
  life (home, beauty, social connection, sex, health,
  transportation, etc.) that are more flexible, less tied
  to a rigid standard? Are you finding this flexibility in
  other areas of life? Who can model freedom from rigid
  standards in your life?

* What would it feel like to let go of, or even reduce the
  pursuit of the things you checked off on the list? How
  would you go about doing that?

* Have you ever done things that you regret as a result
  of chasing the high of escalating sexual or romantic
  relationships, or getting sexual or romantic attention?

* What would help now if you were doing or considering
  doing any of those things?

Accountability: Not Minimizing, Not Punishing

Angel and Fin's relationship has felt strained lately. They are providing live-in care for Fin's grandmother, who is sometimes rude to Angel, and makes sexist remarks to her. Angel feels like Fin should say something. Whenever she tries to bring it up, Fin is defensive. They are both tired, the care work takes a toll on them, and Fin feels like Angel is making a big deal out of nothing. Lately they are finding themselves either not talking much, or fighting about who should do the chores and errands that fill their days.

We live in a society that responds to people being hurt in two ways: either with denial, telling the person who was hurt to shut up; or by casting the person who did the harm as a bad guy who needs to be punished.

Minimization—like Angel is experiencing when Fin dismisses her complaints about Fin's grandmother's sexist remarks—is very common. Because we live in a culture that minimizes harm, most of us are afraid no one will listen to us when bad things are happening. This can cause us to not talk about what's wrong, or it can make us unrelentingly hungry to see harm doers punished, sometimes to the point of insatiability. At the same time, this dynamic makes us afraid to admit any wrongdoing of our own, afraid of blame, retaliation, and punishment. This polarity is a setup—it means we rarely experience right-sized responses to hurt and harm.

What is missing when we live on these two extreme ends of the spectrum is the reality that all people do things that hurt others, and all people experience hurt. The path to reducing hurtful actions in our society is not to blame and punish a few people severely while ignoring most harm. Instead, we need to make room for all of us to learn about the impacts of our actions and how to not repeat things that hurt others. Even though we may fantasize about punishing people who have done hurtful things, we can see that a punishment approach doesn't work. Most people who do the worst harming in our society (bankers, cops, CEOs, soldiers, people who protect institutions where serial sexual assault is normalized) never get punished. Our punishment system instead targets people just because they are poor, disabled, Black, Native, undocumented, queer, or trans. Amid vibrant movements to dismantle police and prison systems, we also need to take apart these ideas inside ourselves, to move beyond blame and vengeance toward compassion, because we know that everyone hurts people, and that anyone can learn to stop doing so.

A punishment-centered society requires numbness, defensiveness, and vengeance. Internalizing these scripts hurts our relationships in the day-to-day and prevents the connections we want and need. It doesn't mean we have to skip over feeling hurt, or that it is bad to feel angry when we are hurt. It means we need to try to shake free from the lies we've been told about "good" and "bad" people that make us deny many kinds of hurt and harm, or seek punishment. One way we can move toward this is to improve our capacity to give and receive feedback with people in our immediate lives, about even small areas of conflict and difference, like those regarding chores, punctuality, and following through on tasks. The more we can practice listening and not minimizing when someone gives us feedback, and sharing feedback with others in a compassionate and measured way rather than being out for blood, the better our skills will be when larger conflicts come up.

Feedback Questionnaire

Being open to giving and receiving feedback is related to our abilities to feel and to participate in resistance movements.

* Recall a time when someone gave you direct feedback and it didn't go well. Perhaps they were harsh, or you were defensive. What went badly? Why?

* Recall a time when someone gave you direct feedback and it went well. Perhaps you were able to learn something useful. Perhaps your relationship with them deepened. What went well?

* Recall a time when you gave someone direct feedback and it went well. What happened?

* Recall a time when you gave someone direct feedback and it didn't go well. What happened?
* Power dynamics impact feedback, for example when people in dominant roles (bosses, parents, teachers, landlords) give feedback but won't receive it, or when people in subordinate roles are afraid of consequences of giving honest feedback. Which of your relationships have the most options for mutual, direct feedback? Are there ways that you could increase possibilities for mutual feedback?
* What helps you receive feedback in ways that strengthen skills, connections, stamina, self-awareness? What would help you offer useful feedback, especially across power dynamics? How do you and the people in your life share preferences for offering feedback?

Giving feedback in small ways, and frequently, means we are less likely to face resentments that blow up. This also flexes our skills of boundaries and differentiation (see Chapters Four and Six). Are there people you could practice sharing small, low-stakes feedback with on day-to-day things? Could you explicitly ask anyone in your life to practice this together with you?

Chasing Cultural Fantasies about
Sex and Romance

Jordan likes giving and getting attention, and often develops huge crushes on someone he flirted with at a party or messaged on social media. It escalates fast—as soon as he gets interested in someone, he starts imagining the two of them together. He'll spend hours searching online for pictures and mentions of them, and trying to figure out who and what they like. His dates often find him too intense, and break it off after a short while. His friends complain about how much drama Jordan's love life creates in their circle. Sometimes Jordan lets himself dream about dating someone long enough to relax and feel comfortable, to just be himself and not have to work so hard.

Our thinking patterns are a product of practice, and we have practiced specific thinking patterns because they helped us get by. The romance myth's messages can set many people up to have too much or even obsessive thinking about people they have crushes on or want to fuck. That might include overthinking things like how to get someone to like you, how to be more attractive, or what your crush or your ex is doing with whom. It makes sense that sex and romance become sites of overly developed fantasizing—some of which feels good and some of which is anxious—because we've been inundated with the message that lovers could make us happy or that being attractive means we are worthy.

For some of us, escapist patterns of thinking can be like an intoxicant. Bored at work? Look at your crush's social media. Stressed about money? Research plans to change your body. Fighting with a friend? Stay up all night on the sex apps. This kind of pattern—using something to get away from whatever is going on right now, whatever you are feeling right now—can be done with almost anything, and things related to sex and romance are prime candidates because they are so loaded with cultural promises of satisfaction. In this world it is often safer not to be present in reality. Our bodies and brains establish genius ways to get a break from the present.

Is this compulsive, addictive, or just fine?

Many of us have compulsive relationships to certain behaviors and activities. By "compulsive," I mean we want to stop or cut back but can't, or are unable to begin a new activity we want for our well-being. Often compulsive activities are related, such as overdeveloped attention to dating and sex impacting sleep, so it can be useful to think about them together.

* Where in your life do you see these imbalances? (e.g., sleep, screen time, shopping, money, schoolwork, etc.)

* What is your self-talk about this like? Another way to phrase this: Are you saying mean things to yourself in your head about these areas of imbalance?
* Do you imagine a certain person or institution telling you the "right" way to act? Would you hold someone you love to this rigid standard?
* What do you do instead of making the change you want? Is there a middle path toward new action? What pleasures can be found in making this change?

It's worth noting that there is so much shame and judgment about sexuality that we have to be careful how we handle this inquiry about possibly compulsive behavior. Something is only compulsive or addictive if we are noticing, for ourselves, that it feels imbalanced or that we want to stop or start and find we can't. It can be difficult, but we have to assess whether we are actually identifying an imbalance, or just using the label "compulsive" to shame ourselves. Talking to a friend can help to sort this out.

Like Jordan in the story above, chasing these cultural fantasies in an imbalanced way can undermine our connections with dates and friends. Figuring out if we are using something in this way, and how that is impacting our lives, is fundamental to improving our relationships.

No Labeling and Judging—Please Don't Weaponize the Ideas in This Book

I encourage you to use the content of this book to understand your own behavior, rather than to scrutinize others. Our puritanical, ableist, criminalizing, racist society encourages us to categorize and judge others, yet deprives us of tools for self-reflection and self-accountability. When another person's behavior impacts us, it is okay to respond, such as limiting contact, reducing trust, or setting other boundaries. But slapping pop psych labels on ourselves or others (like "compulsive," "addict," or "obsession") won't help us build the relationships we need. We can more usefully ask, "Am I being impacted by their behavior such that I need to prioritize my own well-being?" and "What is my responsibility for my well-being, and how can I start there?" Intervening and giving feedback are sometimes appropriate but will be more effective, principled, and grounded if we have started by attending to our own feelings and reactions.

The dominant cultural context requires coping mechanisms that skew our relationships to pleasure, sex, money, food, work, and everything else, so most of us have experienced "compulsion" or "addiction," or even just the ordinary hyperconcentrated attention, and inattention, required to get by. Harmful systems judge, label, and stigmatize imbalanced relationships to some activities (like criminalized drugs) while encouraging imbalanced relationships to others (like work or exercise), and the buffers of money and privilege shape how disruptive having an imbalance will be for different people. Sometimes we use imbalanced behaviors as outlets for escape with fewer difficult consequences. Given all this, it's not useful to label other people as addicts within our efforts at healing.

My aim in this book is not to provide firm criteria for when something is "a problem." Instead, all the ideas in this book are about how to develop emotional skills that support our capacities to feel, understand our reactions, make choices about how to interact with each other, and build strong relationships. There is no clear line of when something is imbalanced, and there are no clear instructions on how to manage our coping mechanisms. All we can do is enhance our capacities to feel and to choose our actions, rather than reacting on autopilot. Inquiry and practice can improve accountability to ourselves and our chances to be of service to others, even when we are around people who are going through crisis.

Getting High

Tafari can't get to sleep at night because he stays up, always later than he intends to, trying to connect on sex apps. He set limits for himself at first—only message with people he intends to meet, stop scrolling when it stops being fun, turn off his notifications after midnight—but he usually breaks his own rules and stays up until 3 or 4 a.m. He knows he needs more sleep, but the thrill of exchanging pics, seeking and getting people's attention, is just so compelling. Every time the notification dings he feels wide awake, and even when he's exhausted he can't seem to put the phone down and go to sleep.

Research shows that we get chemical highs from flirting, having sex, dating, viewing porn, escalating relationships, scanning social media, lying about sex, and other related activities. Serotonin, oxytocin, and other "happy" chemicals increase in the brain because of sex and the experience of falling in love, and even from doing sketchy things or things that feel somewhat unpleasant, like obsessively googling someone who has rejected us.

Both the romance myth and the chemical pathways generated by repeated practice train our brains to seek out highs. We are conditioned to pursue experiences we expect will trigger good or intense feelings. Is any of your behavior related to sex, dating, or relationships driven by chasing highs?

We might get that chemical thrill when we make eye contact with our crush, write that flirtatious message, or confess something about our feelings in order to escalate a relationship.

The highs that come from these activities can be sweet and pleasurable, and these can be appropriate and delightful things to do. But if we are doing things just to get a buzz, even if it makes our lives harder or hurts others, then the desire for this high might be out of balance. For example, someone who escalates relationships because they love the high of having someone confess feelings for them, but who is not sincerely interested in the relationship beyond getting this high, might leave a trail of broken hearts and busted expectations in their community. Or, someone seeking certain highs might just feel like they are out of balance even though their habit or practice isn't hurting others, like how Tafari is tired of missing needed sleep because of chasing approval on the sex apps.

Chasing highs can cause other consequences—like when we fail to complete a project or mess up our schoolwork because we are too distracted by chasing those good feelings. It can also lead to sex we don't really want, flirtation that is misleading, or escalation of a relationship out of proportion to our actual interest. Sometimes we want the immediate boost of chemicals from the excitement or attention without the follow-up implications. Perhaps we can't distinguish between genuinely being attracted to someone and just wanting the high. It can be uncomfortable to look at our motivations, to find out what is driving us, and to examine the impact it is having on us or others.

High-chasing can produce relatively inauthentic connections driven by the romance myth. We might project positive qualities on people to fuel the excitement of getting their attention. We might project excessive negative qualities onto people whom we want to break up with or who have rejected us. Both of these dynamics are part of the reactive cycle of getting self-worth from sexual and romantic attention.

Some of us use political justifications for our iffy behaviors when we are chasing highs. An example might be using normative—or subcultural—values to push relationship agreements or dynamics because we want to get what we want *right now.* This could look like pressuring a partner to change your agreements about how you connect with other dates, ostensibly based on a political commitment to autonomy but actually motivated by an urgent desire toward some particular sexual or romantic activity.

Or it could look like pressuring a partner to escalate a relationship in accordance with the normative romance myth (meeting each other's friends, exchanging jewelry, cohabitation, etc.). Pressuring people to do things they don't want to do in relationships is always concerning, but especially if our motivations don't line up with what we are saying to our lovers. The thrills of getting high from sex and romance happen within a minefield of coercive, shame-based, normalizing ideologies about sex and bodies, so we can really hurt each other and ourselves if we're not aware of our motivations and their impacts.

Many of us also use sex, flirting, and dating to feel desirable. This can make sexuality into a performance, a way to prove our worthiness and get affirmed in our gender and sexual identities. When we are driven by that desire for approval, many of us end up suppressing our preferences and needs in order to deliver an approved-of performance. At its worst, this can include doing things that we don't like, that don't feel safe, or that we regret. Don't get me wrong—it's okay to perform during sex if we want to. It can be liberating and fun to try on new sexual and gender roles, power dynamics, parts, and acts. But sometimes, when sex or intimacy is a performance, it can be an evasion of vulnerability, and an abandonment of ourselves. Examining these patterns and developing clearer boundaries can help us find ways to do more of what we want in this area of life.

Some people chase a whole package of cultural fantasies and emotions in a way that becomes a painfully predictable pattern—one that can deprive their relationships of specificity— slotting new people into the same partner-shaped space over and over. I had a friend who described this as having a "men's room" in her head. She wasn't talking about a toilet. She described how this room in her mind always had some current romantic interest in it or prior partner she was upset about, taking up a lot of her attention. She kept a person in there constantly, and told me she felt immense relief when she finally started to intentionally leave it empty.

The result was that she was able to see people she was interested in more clearly as she got away from the set of mental habits and settings that previously slotted people into this room. By working to become aware of the unconscious patterns through which she became attracted to and involved with romantic partners, she was able to move beyond the reactive scripts that were running her feelings and behaviors, and see people and situations more accurately. This kind of shift can also help us engage with others more respectfully, as we perceive more of who they are rather than only looking for how they can fit into the roles in our scripts.

Addicted to New Relationship Energy?

In her book *Polywise*,[9] Jessica Fern, a therapist specializing in supporting people practicing nonmonogamy, talks about how some people relentlessly chase the thrill of what she calls New Relationship Energy—the chemical and emotional highs that often come at the start of romances (more on the phases of the romance cycle in the next chapter). New Relationship Energy is wonderful and fun, and it is, by nature, temporary. People who seek that phase of relationships again and again tend to leave a lot of drama behind them, because they escalate with each new partner but give no indication that they will likely bail as soon as the relationship leaves that euphoric phase.

There is nothing wrong with wanting relationships of limited duration, or with breaking up when we want to. However, it can become unethical or unkind to repeat a pattern of escalation with partners, chasing the high of making big commitments with each other, and then leaving when the escalation highs diminish. In my experience, most people who perpetuate this dynamic have no idea they're stuck in a pattern. They just feel wildly in love when they make all those escalating decisions with a new lover, and then are genuinely forlorn when things get rocky and they leave the relationship. They don't know that the emotional pattern is one of chasing the high of escalation, rather than falling for the wrong person. Sometimes it takes friends and community members pointing out this repetition of behavior and its impacts to their attention for some New Relationship Energy chasers to begin to see the pattern for what it is.

I am not arguing that the right thing would be for these people to stay in relationships after escalating, or to avoid escalating relationships at all—rather the suggestion here is that we can become more aware of our subterranean motivations and emotional habits. Only by understanding the power romance-myth narratives have over us, and working to see our feelings and actions more clearly, can we find more authentic, consensual ways to connect with lovers in relationships of any duration. This might include an investigation of whether or not we are avoiding the emotional growth that comes with the conflicts that emerge *after* the euphoria of New Relationship Energy (see Chapters Four and Five).

Where All This Chasing Leads

OUR IMBALANCED PURSUITS can lead to many difficult behaviors:

* Ditching friends for dates, prioritizing a new date over everything else
* Dropping responsibilities or making impulsive decisions for a new lover, like moving far away or abandoning safer sex practices
* Being deceptive about sex or dating
* Seeking attention from people without being interested in them

* Hooking up with others for attention, intentionally misleading them
* Agreeing to relationship arrangements you don't want in order to appear to have radical sex politics and no hard feelings (like jealousy) or needs (like reassurance, security, reliability)
* Escalating relationships with people without wanting to, and entering committed relationships without desire
* Escalating with a date/partner to get high, and then talking shit about them with friends
* Pursuing romantic connections in organizations or workplaces where it would likely be more peaceful and supportive to date elsewhere
* Promising yourself after a breakup to take a pause from dating to examine any patterns, but instead ending up immediately involved again
* Violating other people's privacy or boundaries because of an obsession with a person
* After breakups, having big emotional crashes that significantly disrupt activities, or cause harm
* Ditching a date suddenly and/or without communication
* Cycles of escalation, euphoria, conflict, breakup, crash, in consecutive relationships or within one relationship, that cause hard feelings or hurt others
* Gossiping about other people in damaging ways because of strong reactions to a sexual or romantic experience

This necessarily incomplete list identifies common behaviors that many of us have witnessed or engaged in ourselves, that may even seem "normal" in our social circles. These behaviors can lead to increased isolation for people in romantic relationships and contribute to conditions for harm and violence. Some lead to conflict in groups, resulting in members being exiled, important projects and collaborations being lost, and long-term bad blood dividing people who depend on one another.

Chasing romance-myth fantasies and highs can cause us to do unethical things that we later regret. The Icarus Project—a network of peer-support groups dedicated to destigmatizing mental health—created a tool called Mad Maps that helps us prepare for times when we are overtaken by powerful mental and emotional states. The idea is to make a plan when we are *not* in the altered state, and then be able to use it when we need it.

I recommend mad mapping for whatever intense states you get into with sex and romance—obsessive crushing, breakup spiraling, new-relationship escalation overload, the oblivion of a sex app haze—and I have included an exercise about mad mapping jealousy in Chapter Six on p. 307 as an example. If you already know some of the patterns you repeat, you can work on a mad map now that will support you when you find yourself in the storm of those feelings.

The Bottom Lines exercise on p. 301 and the Dating Plan tool on p. 298 are also ways to take what you have learned about what's not working and make concrete plans to put that wisdom to use. There is also a reflection tool on p. 296, based on Reid Mihalko's protocols for people seeking to keep sex "casual" (he developed a list for people who intend to keep sex casual but fall into a more serious connection). Finally, following this you'll find an exercise called Seven Steps for De-Escalating a Crush or Obsession, to use when you have a crush and you want to turn its volume down.

* Can you relate to the idea of getting high from sex, love, dating, flirting, obsessing over relationships or exes? How might these patterns of thinking or behavior impact you or others?
* If you are identifying any imbalances in this area, what do you think is driving them?
* Are there loving, nonjudgmental people who you could talk with about imbalances and with whom you could explore the exercises and questions in this book?

Seven Steps for De-Escalating a Crush or Obsession

Sometimes you have a strong interest in someone who, for whatever reasons, you feel it would be a mistake to pursue. This tool is for when you want to turn the volume down on a crush. Crushes are made of repeated practices. This exercise will help you find out what you are practicing so you can make choices about it, instead of feeling so swept up.

Step 1: What is the reason this feels like something I should de-escalate or stop?

Step 2: What does the current crush practice look and sound like?
When do I fantasize about this person (on the bus, in class, when I listen to music, etc.)? What are my recurrent thoughts about the situation that fit within the romance-myth narrative?

Examples might include:
☐ *I cannot help these feelings.*
☐ *This is the one right person for me.*
☐ *This situation is tragic and inevitable.*
☐ *I will never feel this way about anyone else again.*
☐ *I have to find out how this person feels about me.*
—What else?

Ask yourself:

* What is pleasurable about this experience? What is unpleasant or stressful?

* What, if anything, am I doing that I might regret later (lying, avoiding things that need my attention, escalating, misleading, following them around, etc.)?

* Am I using this crush to meet some particular need, like alleviating boredom at my job, avoiding my partner or family, stimulating my sexual aliveness, or something else?

Step 3: What dream or vision do I have for my life beyond this obsession? What do I want instead?

Check off any of the below that ring true for you, and add your own.

☐ *I want a fun, creative sex life with my partner(s) and/or myself.*

☐ *I want to leave my existing relationship in a loving, graceful way.*

☐ *I want to feel excitement, generosity, and interest in my existing relationship(s).*

☐ *I want to feel desire without shame.*

☐ *I want to have a life with honesty and no deception.*

☐ *I want less jealousy and envy in my life.*

☐ *I want to have clear discernment rather than inflated projections about other people, so I can make choices based in reality.*

☐ *I want to feel secure and supported in my friendships.*

☐ *I want to feel that embracing my desire for excitement, sex, and romance is not at odds with my principles, values, or integrity.*

☐ *I want to show up for my community and friendships by being an honest, reliable person. No deception or sketchy business.*

☐ *I want to feel peaceful and serene, knowing there's no drama.*

☐ *I want to feel more comfortable being alone.*

Step 4: Identifying Hot Spots

Hot spots are the particular times, places, or situations that are precursors to the obsessive thinking or the action we are trying to move away from.

What are your hot spots?

* What forms of communication tend to escalate the crush for you? Are there certain forms of communication where you tend to cross lines you meant to hold, such as texting late at night, communicating when intoxicated,

communicating through social media, or talking in person alone with your crush?

* What feeling states (boredom, intoxication, loneliness, insecurity, etc.) tend to lead to the fantasizing or acting out the crush? What could you do instead when those come up?

* What specific actions are motivated by this crush (going to certain places, reaching out to certain people, etc.) that you can curtail?

Step 5: Using Summary Sentences

When we are caught up in emotional processes like crushes that we think are not benefiting us but feel compelling, we toggle between *self-judgment* and *rationalization* of the behavior. One side says something like, "I'm terrible for having these feelings. I'm going to ruin everything." The other side says, "I can't help what I feel. Maybe this is meant to be." Or the rationalizing side might minimize the behavior, saying "It's not a big deal" or use a justification like "I get to be free and have fun."

What we need is a way to return to a sober assessment of the situation, to remind ourselves of the buzz-kill realities that make this emotional/behavioral pattern something we are trying to break. Killing buzzes may sound like a bummer, but in this case, it's about getting back to reality so we can find actual joy and pleasure rather than drama, shame, and conflict.

Carrying around these summary sentences is a way to snuff out the buzz. Make them short and keep them in a pocket for use when needed.

Examples of summary statements:

* Pursuing this person is going to cause drama and disruption. I can take concrete steps to de-escalate my crush. Being friends with this person is just as valuable as crushing on them, and avoids the drama.
* I'm not available. I want to bring my attention back into my committed relationship. I don't want to hurt myself or my partner or mislead this person.
* I don't actually know this person. I am making stuff up about them, making myself feel obsessed and off-center. I can choose to come back to reality. I want to be in reality, not desperate/high/acting out.
* I have been asked to back off. I can choose to do this and respect myself, the other person, and our community. I want mutual, balanced relationships based in respect.
* The strong feelings I am having will pass. I don't have to act on them. I can make choices to fuel them or to dampen them—I have a choice here.

* This person has told me (or shown me) that they are not available. I can let go and move my attention toward things that will be more satisfying.

Step 6: Making a Plan for Dealing with Hot Spots

A plan for navigating your hot spots can look like this: "When I encounter [hot spot], I will be tempted to [feeling/behavior] and instead I can [new choice that helps me cope in a different way]."

Here are some examples:

* When I am going to sleep, I will be tempted to fantasize about making out with my crush. Instead, I can listen to an audiobook, do a breathing exercise, or think about my adorable dog/cat/iguana.

* When I hear about a party that my crush might be at, I will be tempted to organize my life and my friends around being there. Instead, I can make other plans for that night.

* When I am emailing with my crush about our mutual aid project, I will be tempted to flirt in the email or find a reason we need to meet in person. Instead, I can stick to logistics in the email and not initiate unnecessary in-person meetings.

* When I am visiting my parents, feeling bored and misunderstood, I will be tempted to text or DM my

crush. Instead I can call or message my best friend or my roommate. I can read a novel, listen to podcasts, bake a dessert, or take a walk.

Step 7: Be Gentle
Are you likely to be overly rigorous and self-judgmental? Or do you tend to be more lax, to rationalize maintaining the pattern you have committed to breaking? Keeping your tendency in mind and trying to err on the other side is often helpful.

Waking Up to Reality, or "Being Present"

IF YOU ARE reading this book, you probably know something about how rough times in sexual or romantic connections can disrupt our lives, cause us to act outside of our values, and cause pain. A core idea in this book is that awareness is key to liberation. Noticing allows us to catch the patterned cultural norms and scripts so we can say, "Hey, that's not me, that's not mine!" and make conscious choices.

Rooting out patterns of numbing out and relentlessly chasing romance-myth fantasies and highs leaves us room for what some call *being present*. This phrase may be overused these days in the shallow, corporate mindfulness and wellness industries, but it is one name for the kind of liberation that

I am proposing here. Just as our resistance movements seek to break with the illusions of dominant systems, we need to do similar work in ourselves to wake up to reality, cast off lies, and build what we want. Becoming aware of our feelings, being present to what is making us react and to the impacts of our thinking and feeling patterns, is essential to taking our lives back and becoming the people we need to be in these difficult times.

Right now, even those of us who care a lot about liberation often act our worst in our sexual and romantic relationships, influenced by the romance myth and disposability and scarcity thinking. It's frightening how much conflict and damage our romantic and sexual hijinks can cause in our social circles and in the resistance groups we so urgently need to create and sustain. However, we can increase our emotional awareness and better align our actions with our principles with sustained effort. Investigating where we are stuck on autopilot—chasing empty highs, numbing out, or repeating scripted cycles—is key to finding new kinds of freedom, connection, and pleasure.

The living world is made of relationships; we need each other to survive. Figuring out what is living in us that throws us off balance is essential to finding new ways to live collaboratively. Having seen how norms and scripts, numbness, and the pursuit of fantasies and highs distort our experiences, we can now dive into one of the most prevalent cultural patterns that shapes this area: the Romance Cycle.

Chapter Two Recap

* The systems we live under work to keep us numb and passive. If we are numb to the pain they cause us, and that we ourselves cause others through complicity and complacency, we are easier to control.

* We are taught both to minimize the harm we experience, and to deny and defend ourselves when anyone tells us we hurt them. As a result, most of us are unskilled at giving and receiving feedback, which limits our self-awareness and damages our relationships.

* This numbness is punctuated by a desire to feel fully alive—a feeling we pursue frantically and expect instantaneously. Often we seek to meet it by chasing fantasies and highs fed to us by harmful dominant systems.

* Many of our worst behaviors in sex and romance come from unconsciously chasing instant gratification or by trying to adhere to society's script for the things we should desire, like romance-myth fantasies. This can lead us to unsatisfying patterns that hurt us and others.

* Becoming aware of how we are numbing out and how we are chasing fantasies or highs can help clarify what's not working and what it is that we actually want.

Falling in Love and Losing Your Mind: The Romance Cycle

The true focus of revolutionary change is never merely the oppressive situations which we seek to escape, but that piece of the oppressor which is planted deep within each of us . . .

—AUDRE LORDE, *Sister Outsider: Essays and Speeches*

Aliyah and Fatima each felt like they had finally found someone who understood them. They became inseparable, had hot sex, shared their favorite political ideas together. They felt alive.

Six months in, things started to get tense. Fatima felt like Aliyah was "checked out" or not as in love as Fatima was. Aliyah began to feel like she could never satisfy Fatima and was tired of being criticized for spending time with other people. She felt like she was expected to read Fatima's mind.

The fighting got worse over time, and when they broke up, their friend circle was divided—people took sides. Fatima felt frustrated. She had been through something very similar with her last girlfriend, and couldn't figure out if she was choosing the wrong people to date. Aliyah immediately fell into a fast and furious romance with someone new.

DESPITE HOW UNIQUE we all are, our love, sex, and romantic relationships can follow similar patterns. The systems we live under set up norms and scripts that embed ideas deeply into our psyches about what love and care should feel like and be like. These patterns cause many of us to act our worst toward dates and lovers.

This chapter is about why romantic relationships can stir up such strong feelings and so much conflict. It explores a common pattern in romantic relationships, illustrated by Fatima and Aliyah's story, above: a romance phase full of positive projections, followed by a phase of disappointment, blame, and conflict.[1] This pattern also occurs within friendships and in groups.

At the end of the relationship, Fatima is asking herself, "Why do I keep having relationships that go this way?" She can't tell if there's something she is doing that makes her dates "check out," or if she's too needy, or if she's unconsciously choosing people who can't sustain interest or attention in the ways she wants.

Aliyah may not be asking herself similar questions, because she is caught up in a new affair, but perhaps her friends are noticing that she has been in a string of intense relationships that have ended in conflict. That kind of conflict often causes turmoil in our friend groups, leading to us taking sides. How do we end up in these patterns, and how can we become more aware of them? How can we stop these dynamics from repeating in our relationships? This chapter offers some tools to help.

When I use the word *projection* in this chapter, I'm describing the way we often interpret each other's actions through our prior experiences or our own feelings. Imagine your crush is standing across from you, and you are holding a projector that is shining images on them—as if they are a blank screen. You are seeing them, but you are also seeing your projection—perhaps thrilling fantasies about how perfect, brilliant, and sexy they are, or else, the fear that they will be like a lover who left you or treated you badly in the past.

Projection is generally unconscious. We don't know that we aren't seeing clearly. It might feel reasonable to look for evidence that your new lover has the same qualities as someone who hurt you in the past. It might feel *objectively* true that they are the hottest, smartest, coolest person ever. Unconscious projections can get in the way of us responding accurately to our current situation.

Here's a road map of the pattern we are going to look at in this chapter, which helps explain what happened between Aliyah and Fatima.

The Cycle of Romance

Feeling an attraction rooted in childhood shaping

*

Unconsciously hoping that this person will make you feel loved in the ways you've always longed for

*

Falling in love with the projection that this person will help you recover parts of yourself you had to cut off or deny to get through childhood

*

Ignoring their unappealing qualities

FEELING LIKE YOU "LANDED" THEM

Disappointment that they don't meet your wish fulfillment— they don't love you perfectly, and you feel neglected or trapped or misunderstood

*

Blame, resentment, conflict

Breaking up and doing the cycle again with someone else,
OR
Breaking up and examining what happened in the cycle and having more choice next time you initiate a new relationship,
OR
Cooling off in the relationship and distance or resentment,
OR
Getting stuck in cycles of fighting,
OR
Doing transformative work on yourself and/or within the relationship that can stop the cycle

---

?

---

* Have you ever felt stuck, having the same relationship problems come up again and again, even with new people?

* Have you been in or observed relationships that went through a euphoric phase followed by difficult conflict? Why do you think this happens?

* How do these repeating cycles impact our resistance groups and movements?

Childhood Shaping

Lydia grew up with a very controlling mom who constantly scrutinized and criticized her, made her eat specific things, wear certain clothes, and participate in a packed schedule of activities. If she got excited about something, her mom took over the activity and made it into another area of rigid control. Her mom was unpredictable and quick to anger. To avoid her mom's scrutiny, Lydia became secretive and hid many parts of her life.

In adulthood, Lydia has had trouble connecting and doesn't tell her friends or dates much about herself. She is turned on by secrets and sexual activity that feels illicit. Sometimes sneaking around feels exciting, but she has lost some important relationships because of it. She often dates people who are controlling, and finds it difficult to assert her own preferences or needs, often just going along with whatever they want. In some ways, she feels loved and cared for when people are bossy. However, eventually she starts to pursue sexual activities in secret that feel risky or taboo. With the secrecy comes bad feelings, and ultimately, the relationship becomes overburdened with trust issues.

Luis grew up with his aunt as his caregiver. She was a very social and expressive person. She was unconventional and wild in some fun ways, and also kind of unstable. She would pull him out of school to go on trips with her boyfriends that sometimes put him in uncomfortable or dangerous situations. She would stay in bed for months whenever a relationship ended.

It was stressful for Luis to be on the roller coaster of his aunt's emotional highs and lows. He became a very careful, somewhat constrained person. His life is focused on meeting obligations and being stable, reliable, and responsible. However, he has a hard time feeling genuine desire or excitement about anything. When he was a teenager and in his early twenties, he had some dramatic love affairs with people who were unpredictable, but since then he has felt pretty shut down.

It's a cliché that we get romantically entangled with someone like our parents, yet it is true that we are deeply shaped by early caregivers. Sometimes we are attracted to people because of the ways that they remind us unconsciously of our childhood caregivers (parents, older siblings, grandparents, foster parents). Unconsciously, we hope to recreate a similar situation with a different outcome, perhaps finally feeling loved, cared for, free, understood, or whatever we couldn't find in childhood.[2] We can see how Lydia and Luis were each shaped by their relationships to their caregivers and carry that baggage into adulthood.

Personally, the people I find most compelling mirror the dynamics I was raised in, where I learned what relationships feel like. Examining my own experiences of sex, dating, and romance has convinced me that much of my adult behavior was shaped in my childhood. My primary caregiver was my single mom, who struggled with depression, alcoholism, and the stresses of raising three kids in poverty. She often did not have a lot to give, so I sought connection by trying not to have too many needs, by being charming, helpful, and interesting to her.

I formed the belief that I had to strive to get people to love me. I came to believe that I would only be loved for what I could *do*, rather than being inherently loveable. As a result, I have been drawn to relationships with people (both friends and lovers) who are aloof, where I have to work to get them to open up to me. Whenever I have found that familiar dynamic—of feeling inadequate or having to strive—the experience has felt like a *real*, important, compelling love, even if it also felt bad to do that striving and feel that insecurity in the relationship. When people were more open and generous with love, the relationships felt less intense and captivating.

I have heard this dynamic characterized as having "matching wounds." Relationships where each person's way of being unconsciously stirs up the other's feelings from childhood can be the most intriguing, and also can create the most conflict.[3] I, for example, found the most intensity with aloof partners whose childhood caregivers were overly intervening and controlling. I was unconsciously drawn to the dynamic of having to work to be loved, and they were unconsciously drawn to the fact that I would show a lot of interest, but tended to be controlling when I was insecure. This kind of match— where the most intense attraction activates subterranean feelings from early life—can make relationships more exciting, yet more conflictual, and, potentially, can be an important chance for healing. We can be drawn to friends for the same reasons.

This dynamic is also at play when we meet someone who seems like they should be a great match, but we just don't feel a spark with them. When we pursue a relationship based on less intense initial attraction, it might be less passionate and less troubled, and might end because of disinterest rather than conflict. This is often about us not having the matching wounds that make some relationships so stirring.

This attraction process is not obvious or conscious, and the people we are choosing may not appear like our caregivers in any surface ways, and may not even seem similar to people we've been attracted to before. In fact, people often choose new dates thinking that this person is *so* different from their last partner, only to find themselves with the same troubles. Our emotional settings guide the process of choosing, relating, and reacting in the relationship. Since most of our communication is nonverbal,[4] and our processes of attraction are unconscious, even when we believe we are doing something different, we might be repeating patterns.

We all fundamentally need safety, connection, belonging, and care, and the dynamics that surrounded whoever provided this in childhood (adequately or not) shape our deepest and often unconscious beliefs about relating to others. In adulthood, we continue to play out roles we picked up in childhood (e.g., people pleaser, isolator, worrier, distancer, pursuer, caretaker, boss, etc.). We lead with strategies and feelings we learned in order to get our needs met when we were very vulnerable.

Lydia is attracted to controlling behavior because she learned to love from someone who showed care that way. Being secretive about her interests allowed Lydia some autonomy, and she continues to orient toward secrecy and control even though it causes problems.

Instead of reacting to his aunt's instability by dating similar people, Luis seeks a predictable life even at the risk of chilling his desire. Investigating how those stability-seeking coping mechanisms have become confining might allow him to choose to balance security with more flexibility, creativity, desire, and novelty. We are not eternally bound to the relationship dynamics of our childhood, and the first step in overcoming that conditioning is to notice their presence in our lives.

* Do you notice yourself being drawn to any relationships that echo the patterns of love and security you had with a childhood caregiver?
* Have you projected fears or hopes from prior relationships onto new people? Have you ever noticed someone projecting onto you in this way?
* Have friends ever mentioned observing patterns in your attractions, or how your relationships develop or end?

Falling in Love

Joey and Dev met when they were both volunteering with a prisoner support project. They felt intensely attracted to each other and were soon falling in love. They both felt high for weeks, exchanging texts throughout the day that affirmed their mutual feelings, spending tons of time together almost in a dream state. Even when they planned to spend the night apart, they would often find themselves in a late-night text exchange and one would end up going to the other's house after midnight. It felt irresistible to need one another, and to feel needed.

Dev had struggled with sexual shame and felt liberated with Joey, who was sex- and body-positive. Joey had never felt like a creative person, but Dev was an artist and encouraged Joey to play with art supplies on their dates. Joey felt like a whole new part of herself was opening up from being around Dev's creativity.

In the earliest stages of romantic love, people's euphoric feelings can be fueled by projections that being with this person will finally let them experience wholeness. Unconsciously, we believe that we will be reunited with the parts of ourselves that we had to cut off in childhood. That we will be fully seen and recognized; that we will receive all the love we never got from our initial caregivers.

This intense experience unlocks emotional pathways going back all the way to early childhood: many couples engage in activities and feelings connected with infancy, such as entering a realm of timelessness, staring into each others' eyes, delighting in every inch of each other's bodies, cooing and prattling to each other, using baby names, and desiring and promising to love each other as no one ever has.[5] These activities of early romance can resemble connection behaviors between caregivers and infants, and can play a significant role in showing and feeling closeness.

Through a lover, we may reconnect to the parts of ourselves we had to excise in childhood. In this phase, we may be attracted to the person, at least in part, because they are able to express parts of themselves that we have denied in ourselves. Perhaps we internalized a standard of quietness and retreat, and we are attracted to a person who is loud and willing to take up space. Like Dev in the story above, we may have internalized sexual shame, and so we are drawn to someone who seems more sexually expressive and free. Or like Joey, perhaps we cut off our creativity and now it feels wonderful to connect with someone who expresses theirs and invites us to join.

I remember being nineteen or twenty and going on a date with a new lover. I had grown up poor and spent my childhood trying to hide the fact that my family lived in poverty. One of my adaptations was to cut off certain kinds of desire that I worried would make me look desperate or needy for anything.

I felt—and still sometimes feel—shame about appearing to be trying to get anything for free, or eating first or more than others. I took on the sometimes conscious, sometimes unconscious habit of trying to appear casual, not needing or wanting anything too much. My date had also grown up poor, but coped with it in a different way. We entered the restaurant and grabbed the only empty table, which still had half a glass of wine and a half-eaten dessert from the previous patrons. As fast as she could, she drank the wine and downed the dessert with a look of mischief, joy, and victory on her face.

I was delighted, seeing her boastfully perform this demonstration of appetite and of victory by getting something for free. She didn't care what people thought of her eating strangers' leftovers. Being close to someone performing behavior I would be very ashamed to do myself felt freeing and exciting. I admired a part of her that was liberated, which was not yet free in me.

Our projections are not limited to the other person's positive traits, though. We also might find relief in seeing the other person's "negative" traits.[6] They might express anger, rage, unpredictability, moodiness, neediness, or other traits that we are drawn to precisely because these have been on our internal, unconscious taboo list. They can express the emotions we have denied to ourselves, and unconsciously long for.

During this early romantic phase, we may at times project onto our partners the feelings of necessity we experienced in early childhood with our caregivers. We might feel like we can't survive without this person, even if we know that doesn't make logical sense since we might have only recently met them.[7] Countless love songs relate this theme of desperation about a new lover.

In romantic relationships, people sometimes generate intense emotional emergencies and demands that seem like a matter of life and death, sometimes called "four in the morning" demands. The intense urgency indicates that we are playing out emotional patterns from childhood, where our relationships to our caregivers *were* a matter of life and death. The catchphrase "if it's hysterical, it's historical" captures how these feelings of urgency are based in childhood experiences but are being played out in adult relationships. This level of urgency is relatively typical, but it's also a distortion of reality. Someone's life-or-death feelings do not mean they are going to die, or that their lover *must* capitulate. Even within these compelling "emergency" feelings we can choose, relate, seek support, and find understanding. (More on that in Chapter Four.)

Not only do we project that our romantic partners will fulfill unmet childhood needs, but we also act in ways that support this projection. In a new relationship we might put on a show, cleaning the house for a date, cooking special meals, ditching other obligations in order to spend time with the new lover. In this period of generosity and accommodation, we may even unconsciously act in ways they prefer, and selectively overlook incompatibilities. Without intent to deceive, we collaborate eagerly to fulfill projections and fantasies that don't ultimately turn out to be durable arrangements. The generosity and exuberance of early romance prompt us to give so much care, exchange so much communication, and show such lovely parts of ourselves, that it's necessary to know and anticipate that this phase rarely endures. This isn't because anyone "has changed" or is being intentionally deceptive—it's simply a common part of the cycle.

- * Have you ever been enamored with someone because they had qualities that you couldn't access (e.g., creativity, sexual freedom, exuberance, humor, or adventurousness)?
- * Or because they express emotions you had cut off (e.g., rage, fear, or grief)?
- * If so, what was it like to be around them?
- * Have you ever felt the kind of emotional urgency about a new lover described above, or been on the receiving end of it, or supported a friend who was going through it? What was it like?

Denying Parts of Ourselves and Performing False Selves

Sarita grew up in a family where there was a lot of explosive fighting and violence. She never gets angry, and when other people are angry or upset around her, she feels extremely calm and steady. This has served her well in some situations, but she can also tell that it is limiting her ability to connect. Some of the people closest to her interpret her calmness—when they are upset about something, or in a moment of stress—as distancing, withholding, or even condescending.

Childhood experiences can result in blocked access to certain feelings. Perhaps you were left alone too much in early childhood, so you suppressed the feeling of loneliness. To feel it would have been too devastating. You might come into adulthood unable to feel loneliness or to miss people when you're apart from them. Or you might have formed such a deep groove of loneliness that no matter who you are with, you feel alone. We all have some coping mechanisms that are baked in from childhood and distort our perception of, or ability to be responsive to, current conditions.

We also limit our emotional ranges because of cultural norms, or to accommodate parents who are unresponsive or insecure.[8] Cultural messages about acceptable and unacceptable emotions often enforce race, class, ability, and gender norms. For example, women and girls are often discouraged from responding with anger; Black people are taught early on in life that showing anger will put them in emotional or physical danger; men and boys are frequently discouraged from expressing sadness and vulnerability and encouraged to respond to pain and sadness with stoicism and/or aggression. We grow accustomed to feeling some things and not others, and may not notice these limits, or may think they are our nature.

We lose parts of ourselves, coming to believe when we are young that there are certain things we "can't do." We may hear people say things like "I'm not good at emotions," "I can't relax," "I can't sing," or "I can't think clearly." These kinds of experiences may still be possible for us, but something about our childhood has caused us to cut them off. Sex and relationship therapist Harville Hendrix, describing the romance cycle in his book, *Getting the Love You Want*, asserts that these lost parts of ourselves "are not gone; we still possess them. But for the moment they are not part of our consciousness, and it is as if they do not exist."[9] Raised in families and cultures with negative messages about sexuality and gender, yet living in bodies capable of strong pleasurable sensations, we may also have come to believe that to be a good kid (or specifically a "good boy" or "good girl"), we had to disown certain body sensations or desires.

Childhood teaches us how we need to act to retain the attention, favor, and care of the people who literally held our lives in their hands. And this kind of childhood shaping is powerful. We internalize the norms and enforce the "rules" we have learned, constructing an inner imaginary parent, sibling, teacher, or other authority to police them. We feel anxious and push the forbidden thought or feeling away and, as a result, lose access to important parts of ourselves and thus find our capacities diminished.[10] Early in our lives, as we try to win or retain the care we need from powerful adults, we construct the numbness and the limits on our emotional ranges that were discussed earlier.

In addition to cutting off parts of ourselves, we also produce a *false self* to camouflage the parts that we had to repress.[11] For example, someone who did not get enough support and love in childhood might construct a narrative of self-sufficiency and independence, believing "I can do it on my own," or conversely, might exaggerate problems and pain to get attention. Someone whose caregiver did not allow them to safely explore their autonomy and independence might adapt by forming a belief that they aren't good at things and need a lot of help. People form these false selves in all kinds of creative ways as a matter of survival. Mostly, we don't remember forming them.

In addition to cutting off parts of ourselves and forming a false self, we also may create what Hendrix calls a *disowned self* in this process, acquiring some traits that others may consider negative or difficult. Lydia formed habits of lying and hiding that she was not fully aware of, which sometimes hurt other people and limited her ability to form and sustain relationships. In order to maintain a positive self-image, many of us deny negative parts of our own coping mechanisms.[12]

Nathan Shara, a somatic therapist and teacher, suggests that when we notice difficult traits in others, whether they are lovers, collaborators on a project, or friends or family, we should cultivate more compassion by acknowledging that "they came by it honestly." Most of our annoying or frustrating traits were acquired to survive difficult experiences when we were at our most vulnerable. Our coping mechanisms are not *who we are*.

Having arrived in adulthood with unconscious but often rigid limits on how we can feel, what we can do, and who we can be, we may find ourselves perpetually unsatisfied in relationships but not sure why we can't find what we want. We may lack companionship and connection. In groups, we may struggle to feel a sense of belonging. We may feel overwhelmed by others' needs and struggle to retain connections because of a desire to get away. We may feel envious of others' ways of thinking, feeling, and relating, which seem out of reach to us. We may try to fix an emptiness or numbness or a grasping to feel better through imbalanced relationships to drugs, alcohol, food, work, exercise, social media, other people, sex, or anything else that temporarily distracts us or eases the discomfort.[13]

* What feelings are difficult for you to feel? What experiences might have formed those limits?

* Are there capacities you had to cut off to survive childhood, such as enthusiasm, sexual pleasure, curiosity, trustingness, exuberance, goofiness, sensitivity, seriousness, or others? What taught you to limit certain parts of yourself?

* Are there false selves you had to develop to get attention, be cared for, or avoid punishment? What traits did you have to overperform to get by?

* Are there "disowned self" parts you developed to get by that are still uncomfortable to look at, such as dishonesty, selfishness, cruelty, or controlling behavior?

Leaving the Honeymoon Phase

After three months of wonderful intensity, Dev and Joey started to hit some bumps in the road. It's much easier for Dev to walk to their co-op job from home, so they always wanted Joey to sleep over to avoid taking two early morning buses from Joey's neighborhood. They both enjoyed spending most nights together, and neither of them wanted to be the one to change that and risk losing intimacy and closeness. But Joey's roommates had been complaining that Joey was neglecting her dog by spending so much time at Dev's house.

At first, they were both flexible, with Dev sometimes taking a cab to Joey's, or Joey asking her roommates to care for the dog, but it became harder to compromise. Joey initially admired Dev's dedication to the co-op, but now she sometimes feels frustrated that Dev works so much. Dev had worked less than usual to prioritize being with Joey, but now they are behind and working extra to catch up. Dev feels like Joey doesn't really understand the pressure they are under, since Joey works a job she doesn't care about and never works beyond her set hours.

The phase of romantic euphoria and positive projection that many people experience as "falling in love" isn't meant to last. This tends to shift when we move from imagining how wonderful it will be if we can form this relationship to believing we've formed it. This might happen when we start relying on spending time together, give the relationship status a name, move in together, or become monogamous. What makes it feel like the relationship has been "landed" varies from person to person and is not always logical or conscious.

If this shift happens, the projections will shift, too. Romantic love feeds on fantasy. When the initial high wears off, there is an ordinary person there with gaps, faults, needs, and distortions alongside the qualities we admired so much during courtship.

This shift from a dreamy love story into resentment, annoyance and, too often, mistreatment, brings the cut-off selves discussed above into a new kind of light. The very behaviors and traits you found delightful in your early courtship—that made you unconsciously feel like you might get to have a whole self—are the same ones you later find annoying or even intolerable. Once you exit the phase of wish fulfillment and start to feel like you belong to each other, you apply the same taboos to one another that you've applied to yourselves. You might become embarrassed by, critical of, or annoyed at that sexual expressiveness, loudness, anger, or shamelessness that before had seemed so appealing.[14] Previously admirable career ambition becomes frustration at how much your lover works. That endearing dedication to their family becomes resentment at having to spend vacation and weekend time babysitting their sibling's kids, or visiting elders.

Dev and Joey initially loved spending tons of time together. But now both start to feel resentful that they don't get enough time alone or with other friends, or that their responsibilities are falling by the wayside. Joey feels like Dev is suddenly pulling away when they have to go attend to a backlog of obligations that they put aside during the heat of courtship.

In the new phase, both partners also tend to become less generous. It is difficult to sustain the level of attention and care we give while courting. Once we feel we have won over the lover, the heroic efforts of courtship—elaborate meals, spotless apartments, all-night sex, carefully chosen outfits, undivided attention, abundant texts, and endless availability—start to compete with the daily demands of life. There is nothing inherently bad about this transition; relationships change, and there is great pleasure, connection, and healing available in the phases that follow courtship. However, the shift can provoke conflict and blame.

Disappointment and resentment can rush in, since our romantic projections had us unconsciously expecting to get all our needs met, to be loved like we never were before. An inner wounded child, who might be quite self-centered, can feel betrayed and let down. Gradually or abruptly, we feel less generous, and more aware of which of our needs are not getting met. Many couples have less sex, give fewer backrubs, enjoy less intimate conversation, and instead find themselves watching TV, scrolling social media, or otherwise checking out when they are together.

As we begin to feel more resentment and annoyance, we may treat our partners how our parents or caregivers treated us in childhood. We default to our familiar repressive tactics: shaming, critical messages, punishment, silence, or distance. The negative traits of the other person that we (perhaps unconsciously) ignored or denied can now become glaring.

Often, we feel resentful toward others for not meeting our needs, even though we have not explicitly stated those needs or requests. We unconsciously feel entitled to have those needs met, or project that the other person is intentionally denying us. This is when those "four in the morning" demands often surface.[15] Rather than being demanding, some of us erect emotional barricades, unconsciously feeling that the person we initially perceived to be a source of need gratification is betraying us.[16]

These projections (the euphoric wish-fulfillment ones and the proportionate disappointment ones that come next) can cause us to feel more sensitive and inflexible with our lovers than we would to others, for example being more hurt if the person says no to a request than if a friend were to say no. These feelings may have less to do with the actual person and more to do with our histories and cultural baggage about sex and romance. This shift toward disappointment, resentment, fear of pain, and emotional barricading can lead people to feel anxious or avoidant around their lover. However, if we know that the honeymoon phase is inevitably temporary, we can work to build skills for navigating the terrain of conflict that often follows it. Chapters Four, Five, and Six focus on those skills.

Entering the Conflict Phase

Kila has consistently complained—no matter who they date—that their partners are unwilling to commit sufficiently. For Kila, friends and lovers never seem to show up enough, to give enough. Kila was often ignored and neglected in childhood and dreamed of growing up and finding someone who would love them the way they craved to be loved, noticing everything about them, praising them, anticipating their needs, putting them first in every way. Now, no matter how a partner tries to show Kila love and care, they never really feel it land.

Denise, Kila's current partner, grew up in a strict religious community. She deeply craves autonomy, independence, and to be loved for who she is. She feels trapped, or like she is not good enough, if those close to her ask for more than she is prepared to give. Kila tries to show love for Denise by telling her how much she needs her, or asking what she did that day, or how she feels about something at work, but Denise feels surveilled and becomes more guarded. In contrast, when Denise says she wants Kila to have plenty of autonomy, that they don't need to tell her anything, Kila feels unloved and insulted, like Denise can't be bothered to care. They are each very invested in the relationship, but often bristle at the other's words or feel misunderstood.

Kila and Denise have the "matching wounds" attraction described earlier in this chapter. They have each chosen a partner who will make them feel the familiar stresses of their childhood settings. As their relationship moves past the courtship phase, the conflict surfaces.

Kila believes a romantic partner will make them feel closely held and cared for. Denise believes a loving partner will help her feel free, autonomous, and independent, loving her for expressing who she really is rather than trying to contain or control her. Denise's autonomy makes Kila feel neglected, and Kila's desire for more attention makes Denise feel smothered and controlled.

Part of what draws them to each other is this tension—it undergirds the exciting feelings of romance. Trapped in the romance myth of thinking a lover is like them or can read their minds, they then feel distressed and disappointed when the other person says things that make them feel misunderstood, unloved, smothered, or disconnected, or fails to say the things they most long to hear. Now that the honeymoon is over and conflict is happening, they are finding out how different they are, and that what they want to hear from a lover is not necessarily what the other wants to hear from them.

Urgent Demands, Agitated Emotions, and Accusations in the Conflict Phase

WE HAVE ALL seen beloved friends acting their worst in conflicts with lovers. Perhaps we are surprised by harsh and judgmental things they wouldn't likely say about someone else, petty bickering, or intense urgency and demands. And to further complicate matters, these ways of acting can provoke in partners the kinds of responses that will confirm those projections and maintain the activation of old wounds.[17] Just when we are our most insecure and showing it, our partner might tell us they need space or might call us needy. Just when we are feeling the most trapped and engulfed by a partner, they might get very mad that we're canceling plans or not responding to messages. In this way, we can spin into a mutual dynamic of escalating stress and conflict.

In my early thirties I started a new relationship that became a big part of my life. Around six months after I had asked him to be my boyfriend, he went away to work at a summer camp for two weeks and we were out of touch. I found myself having very bad insomnia during that time, which surprised me. In general, our relationship had a lot of separateness: we hung out with separate friends a lot, and I often traveled for work for long periods. I didn't think I would mind his absence, though I had some mild jealousy knowing there were tons of hot queer people working together at this camp.

When he came back, I found myself feeling uncomfortably desperate for his company. One night, many people who had been working at the camp were passing through town on their way back to their lives, and were gathering at a bar. I joined the group and felt uncomfortable. Usually, I liked that at parties we would flit around talking to different people, but here, I felt stressed and even a bit offended or angry that he was focusing on others. I was very embarrassed to be having these reactions and wanted to hide them, but could not contain myself and left the bar, to my shame, in a bit of a huff.

This experience, I came to realize, was about the activation of this childlike insecurity stirred up by his absence, and my unconscious sense of dependency on him. I was so uncomfortable because my reaction felt out of sync with the spacious, socially promiscuous relationship style we had agreed to. I felt needy, desperate, and possessive, and acted out by criticizing and withdrawing.

If our childhood fears and reactions are stirred up, we might act like children. Babies and little kids, when frustrated, attempt to provoke the people around them, seeking as much attention as possible until someone comes to the rescue.[18] "Always" and "never" accusations tend to arise when people are in this regressed state. "You never clean the house." "I always have to initiate sex." "You never compliment me anymore." Always/never language can indicate that our childhood fears are running the show.[19]

DO YOU RECOGNIZE yourself in some parts of the romance cycle pattern I am describing but not others? Do you recognize parts of it in the behavior of people around you? It's okay if it's not an exact match. This is a rough sketch of an arc of romantic connection that is common enough to cause distress in many people's lives, one that often impacts workplaces, families, social movement groups, and friend circles. Recognizing this arc can generate compassion, and help us make more intentional choices. If we can know where our strong feelings originate, we can navigate them with less blaming, shaming, judging, or gossiping.

* Has there been a particular moment in relationships where you feel like you've secured the relationship, like you are really together now? What does it feel like before, during, after?
* Can you recall moving from a romance phase to a conflict phase with a friend, partner, collaborator, or group? How did your perspectives on them change?

The Cycle:

HOW WE MOVE FROM ROMANCE TO CONFLICT

Unconscious activity	How it shows up during romantic phase	How it shows up during conflict phase (often leading to feelings of avoidance or insecurity)
Projecting denied parts of self onto partner	Partner has it, I admire it, feel freed by being around it, inspired by being with them	Shame that partner has it, disgust or blame, criticism
Connecting to infantile parts of ourselves	Baby talk, timelessness, pet names, extended eye contact, delight in each other's bodies	A feeling that things are "always" or "never" happening, insatiability, tantrums
Wish fulfillment about the love I never got	This partner will give me the love I've always longed for, naturally and easily	Disappointment, blame, and criticism when they don't deliver it perfectly; anger that they can't read my mind; thinking they are intentionally hurting/withholding
Generosity	Special generosity, effort and attention during courtship	Reduced generosity, feeling rejected, disappointment or criticism, resentment, and withholding
Perceiving unappealing traits of the partner	Both people downplay or don't notice unappealing traits.	Unappealing traits are suddenly glaring.
Core survival feelings	I want you so much I could die! (Urgent desire that often feels great, especially when reciprocated.)	You not loving me the way I want is so terrible I could die! (This might show up as an urgent need to get away, or to have more contact. See Chapter Four.)

We can imagine how this pattern I'm describing might escalate as a couple like Dev and Joey continue in it. Perhaps, as Joey complains more about Dev working too much, Dev starts to feel more withdrawn, thinking "I can't ever do enough for Joey, she doesn't appreciate how hard my job is." Joey feels even more alone when Dev withdraws, and keeps bringing up concerns about how much Dev works and that they don't spend enough time together. Eventually Dev storms out of the house, saying "I'm going to sleep at home," confirming Joey's fears of abandonment. When Dev gets quiet and withdrawn during their time together, Joey sometimes feels afraid that Dev is full of rage. Although Dev has not expressed rage, Joey remembers the quiet before the explosion of anger and violence from her dad.

Sometimes a partner's behavior, whether actually similar to a caregiver's conduct or just reminiscent of it, may elicit a fear-driven response, which in turn provokes responses that perpetuate the activation and conflict. When Joey's anxiety about Dev withdrawing manifests in Joey criticizing Dev's work schedule and questioning Dev's commitment, Dev retreats further and Joey's anxiety is further stoked. By working to look at the pattern, Joey and Dev might both be able to get out of autopilot behavior, so that Dev doesn't reactively distance and Joey doesn't fearfully criticize in an attempt to bring some kind of connection back. Chapters Four and Five will examine this type of conflict—where one person

distances and the other person both pursues and criticizes—
and how to navigate it.

The Romance Cycle Shows Up in Nonromantic Relationships, Too

THIS CYCLE CAN happen in any relationship: different versions play out in our friendships, collaborations, and when
we join or form groups. The feelings are frequently most
apparent in romantic and sexual relationships—perhaps in
part because of how the romance myth generates particularly
intense expectations about those kinds of relationships. But
this cycle of projections and disappointment causes plenty of
damage between friends and collaborators and within groups,
and we can benefit from identifying how we are playing it out
in those relationships as well as in sexual ones.

Many of us experience a crash after projecting overly positive qualities and expectations on a new friend or a group
we are joining. Some of us are generous with new people and
groups in ways we can't sustain, leading to disappointment.
Some of us, when we find that a person or group doesn't meet
our hopes, then experience inflated negative projections and
begin to see that same person or group as the enemy, someone
we must trash-talk and campaign against.

Just as we bring our longings to be loved and seen and
appreciated to our lovers, we bring these to friendships, collaborations, and groups. Many people joining resistance

groups hope they will *finally* meet people who understand them and believe in the same things. When differences inevitably arise, they feel betrayed in a way that is proportional to their overblown hopes for belonging. This can be particularly acute if we have often been excluded from groups because of our identities, and we think we have finally found "our people." Identifying this cycle can help us navigate our challenging experience when it comes up.

* Have you experienced or witnessed the romance cycle in a friendship, collaboration, or with a group? What happened? What would you do differently?
* Have you experienced this cycle with lovers, partners, or dates? How does it feel recognizing that this is a common pattern, not just something that you went through?
* What could projects, groups, or organizations do to strengthen group dynamics to weather the storm of these cycles?

Navigating the Conflict Phase

Recently, Dev said they wanted to stay at home alone to get good sleep and be at work on time, and Joey reluctantly agreed. At 11 p.m., though, they were on the phone, with Joey so upset about whether their relationship was okay, and feeling so insecure, that she demanded Dev come over immediately to prove their love for her, because how could they let her suffer like this? Dev was exhausted and worried about money, but resentfully took a cab to Joey's, and spent an anxious night next to her with neither feeling connected.

Understanding more about the romance cycle helps us realize that, as with Joey, our all-consuming feelings are not entirely (sometimes not much at all) about the other person. In fact, we see people we are falling for less clearly than almost anyone else. Hendrix observes, "People in love are masters at projection. Some couples go through their whole marriages as if they were strangers sitting in a darkened movie theater, casting flickering images on each other. They don't even turn off their projectors long enough to see who it is that serves as the screen for their home movies."[20]

Even though we just met, we might cancel other plans for our new lovers, go on dates that end up lasting whole weekends, engage in impulsive future planning, rely on them as a key emotional support, go into debt spending money on them or with them—in other words, overextend ourselves. These behaviors can be thrilling, but they can also isolate us from friends. With practice, we can make choices that are balanced, even when we are having strong, exciting feelings.

For some people, it can help to make guidelines based on our previous experiences of how we go off the rails. (See the Bottom Lines exercise, p. 301, and the Dating Plan tool, p. 298, for aid in navigating this period.) The truth is, falling in love—with a lover, but also sometimes with a friend or with a group we're joining—is something like a pleasurable yet risky intoxicant. Just as people plan their psychedelic mushroom trips to help keep them safe and fun, we can map, plan, and think about how to keep some boundaries and a sense of reality as we start new relationships. (See the discussion of mad mapping jealousy on p. 307.)

Knowing that it is common to experience emotional emergencies in romantic relationships can help us have compassion for ourselves and others, and remind us that we are likely not in as much danger as those alarm bells are signaling. When someone has childhood fears activated and is taking it out on their date, perhaps by making accusations ("You never call me back!" "You've changed!" "You don't prioritize me!" "You always say I'm not doing enough!"), my friend Colby usefully describes it as "throwing their screaming baby" at their lover. It is said as a joking exaggeration, but it is a vivid image. We can learn to recognize when our screaming baby is showing up, and rather than throwing it at people, figure out how to soothe it.

The high-stakes nature of romantic relationships in our society contributes to the panicked feelings that can come up in these conflicts and cause us to act out. The heteropatriarchal romance myth tells us that marriage is the ultimate—or even the only—legitimate option. This suggests that there is something wrong with us if we don't get married. But marital relationships are created under conditions of coercion, not free choice: our legal and social structures put enormous pressure on people to *be* married. Whether people marry or not and whether they stay married can determine their health insurance, taxes, housing, immigration status, income, access to their kids, and other matters of safety and survival.

For centuries, the law made it very hard to get out of marriages at all, especially for women. And even in the twenty-first century, it still isn't easy or cheap. These material conditions and the beliefs and emotional norms they helped create, along with the romance myth and our projections that our partners should fill the roles of our childhood caregivers without whom we will die, can make it hard to even consider leaving a relationship. But if you can't choose to leave, if the relationship is not voluntary, if you feel you don't have options, the emotional conditions are unlikely to improve.

It is useful to remind ourselves that, with rare exceptions, we *can* leave the relationship and survive, and we *can* survive if we are left. The distortions of life-and-death feelings can make it hard to realize this. Remembering that relationships are a choice, and then choosing how to interact rather than desperately clinging, can improve the situation. However, having witnessed couples who constantly threaten each other with breakup, keeping each other emotionally heightened, I would recommend seeking a middle path. The strategy is to remind ourselves and each other that the relationship is a choice, not to threaten others or deliver ultimatums to provoke or coerce outcomes.

Reminding ourselves that we can survive any relationship ending (us leaving, or us being left) requires remembering that other people outside the relationship love and support us. It might also require enhancing our friendships if we have become isolated in our romantic relationships. (For more on why building robust support systems is essential for improving our sexual and romantic relationships, see Chapter Six.)

If you feel like you can't survive your relationship ending, you might try using the What Else Is True? worksheet (p. 48) to get some perspective. In these moments, scarcity mentality might have a hold of you, telling you that you won't find the sexual or romantic partners you want if you leave this relationship. It's true that social hierarchies make some people have easier times than others finding sexual and romantic partners that they want. But it's essential to remember that this scarcity is frequently overemphasized, courtesy of the romance myth and our own emotional activation.

It can help to try to cultivate a sense of ourselves as separate from our partner, held in the web of our other relationships, including our relationship with the natural world and our interests and passions. We can consider what kinds of friendships, interests, and activities we desire to cultivate so that our lives are full of many things, not *just* a romantic partner. Life-or-death feelings are just feelings, not reality, and they will pass. We don't have to judge ourselves for having these feelings, and we don't have to act on them.

In Chapters Four and Five, we will explore how this panic arises in conflict and how we can work through it intentionally. But it is essential to keep in mind that these dynamics are not a sign of anyone's personal failings. Rather, they are large cultural constructs that script our internal lives and lead to predictable, painful conflicts, at least until we build enough awareness about them to instead make authentic, principled choices about how we relate to one another.

* Have you ever been in a relationship where you or someone else made "four in the morning" demands? What was it like to make those demands or receive them?
* Have you ever been afraid or reluctant to leave a relationship? Have you ever been in relationships where there was a breakup threat on the table frequently? What was that like?

Rebuilding Warm Connection:
A Tool for Navigating the Conflict Phase[21]

If you've gotten to the phase with a lover, roommate, or friend where the generosity has worn away and resentment and disappointment have taken over, this exercise can help. Telling each other specific things to make you each feel loved can build emotional connection and satisfaction. It starts with figuring out for ourselves what makes us feel loved. Here are some examples. (Some may be most relevant to romantic relationships, some to other types of relationships.):

I feel loved when you . . .

* Text me to say goodnight
* Cook for me
* Bring me flowers
* Get me a special treat at the grocery store
* Have a leisurely breakfast with me on a weekend morning
* Take me on an adventure that you have planned
* Massage my shoulders
* Ask me about my day when we see each other
* Celebrate birthdays and other important dates with me
* Put away your phone, make eye contact and talk to me when we are reunited after being apart
* Hold my hand

* Ask me about what I am reading
* Compliment my appearance
* Grab me in a sexy way while we are doing chores
* Cover me with a blanket when I am reading on the couch
* Notice and thank me when I do particular tasks

Each person can agree to do two to four of these things per week. The giving must be done freely—not as an exchange for having received something from the other person. It is important for each to know there isn't a price tag.

This activity can help us renew loving feelings and calm the panic that can emerge in the conflict phase, even though we know we are doing an exercise. It can help us see each other as a source of nurturance again, rather than a threat. This exercise also helps amend the naive belief that our partners can read our minds. It offers an opportunity to shift away from the tit-for-tat mentality and break cycles of ungenerosity, resentment, and withholding.

Many of us have a hard time knowing what we really want and like. We may have feared and suppressed pleasure to avoid shame or punishment from repressed caretakers. We learned that to be fully alive was dangerous. This repression may make it challenging for us to come up with requests, and we may then even sabotage our partners' efforts to meet them. It is okay to experiment by putting things on the list, seeing how they feel, and changing them as you learn what lands with you.

People with overbearing or intrusive parents often can't think of asks for this list because it was safer in childhood to hide their desires, even from themselves. It can also be stressful to get what we want. Many of us have pursued people who we knew would not give us what we want. Sometimes we just don't know how to receive the love and care we crave. It can feel like we are violating a taboo to be offered pleasurable care, even if we requested it.

Sometimes the first things people think to put on the list are sites of resentment and criticism, like dishes, laundry, or frequency of sex. However, it is better to start with things that are not at the center of conflict, and also to consider whether those more loaded asks would truly make you feel loved and cared for, or whether instead listing them is motivated by resentment or intended as criticism. Another tendency to avoid is that of listing things that are too vague or general, like "be nice to me." Specificity is key to this exercise.

Breaking Up

For the past six months, Dev and Joey have been having a very hard time. They fight frequently about things like dog care, where they will sleep, why they aren't having sex, and how much time they spend together. Sometimes they have breakthroughs and feel tender and forgiving toward each other; and in these rare moments they remember everything they loved about the relationship.

Dev's best friend, Juan, thinks they should break up. He feels protective of Dev when he hears about Joey criticizing Dev for working too much, and he feels worried that the relationship makes Dev feel inadequate. He is also worried that Dev feels pressured into sex because Joey sees Dev's lack of desire as evidence that Dev doesn't love Joey anymore. Juan is tired of Dev being so upset in this relationship and sometimes gets impatient.

Joey, for her part, is scared that Dev will end the relationship, and often asks Dev to promise not to break up. Dev is on an emotional roller coaster: some days they feel dejected about the situation; some days they experience hurt and anger; other days they fixate on how in love they were with Joey in the past and how badly they want to get that feeling back.

When things get hard, like they have with Dev and Joey, we can do emotional work with ourselves and with each other to try to transform conflict and strengthen our connections. That work might include:

* Building emotional awareness about what we are feeling and thinking when in heightened states
* Building awareness about how we are projecting on others
* Learning to explicitly ask for what we want and listen for what others are asking
* Examining how the romance myth is shaping our expectations and shifting away from it to a more consensual, values-based approach
* Connecting with a bigger support system to help us through the stress of conflict
* Practicing connecting with ourselves to sort out what we really want and don't want (see Chapter Four)
* Doing repair work together (see Chapter Five)
* Learning new ways of communicating when things are hard, such as Nonviolent Communication (see p. 241)
* Reading and reflecting on books about relationships alone or together, or going to therapy alone or together

If everyone involved wants to do this work together and has enough grounded hope that things might get better, a lot of transformative change can happen. Anything that stirs our oldest wounds can bring new life and healing to them. Conflict can be an opportunity for emotional and relational growth, and can generate experiences of feeling deeply loved and understood. However, in some situations, leaving a relationship can be the best path toward growth and healing.

The ways we project on our lovers in the course of the romance cycle can be an obstacle to clear discernment when we are considering whether or not to end a relationship. Often, when I talk with friends who are avoiding breakup, they seem hung up on a positive experience they had (often at the beginning) in the relationship. For example, they describe having had better sex, better communication, more political alignment, or greater growth with this person than any prior partner. This thinking can indicate a belief that your own capacities to connect, express yourself, feel belonging, share who you are, be vulnerable, and feel sexually liberated come from your partner(s).

In fact, *you* created these experiences with this person—these are capacities you have for feeling and connecting. You can replicate or expand these sensations in other relationships or in other contexts—your current lover is not the only portal through which you can experience profundity. Thinking that our lovers are the source of our feelings—good or bad—is common, but it isn't the whole story, and it clouds our ability to see ourselves and our relationships clearly. Sometimes fixating on good feelings or experiences from earlier in the relationship, and hoping they will return, can keep people from considering breaking up when they should.

Of course, repair is possible, and sometimes people work out ways to get their kindness or sexual spark or intellectual connection back. But we must be honest with ourselves about the conditions of the relationship and about our expectations, and make a sober assessment about the degree of work it would take to restore the elements we desire. And in general, we should never stay in a relationship based on the expectation that someone else will change in a specific way we want them to. People grow and change, but not in prescribed or predictable ways.

Should We Break Up?

NO ONE CAN answer this question for you. When you have developed intimacy, experienced heightened emotions, and formed expectations or hopes for satisfying deep desires, it isn't easy or clear when to leave. Leaving means losing some things we want or hope for, and staying means living with some things we don't like. Ask yourself, am I staying based on:

* A belief that this person is going to change and be something they are not right now?
* A fear of being alone, being undesirable, or other sense of scarcity?
* What other people will think of me if I leave?
* An idea that the relationship will revert to feeling the way it once did, even though it's been a while?
* A hope for some feeling or experience that it has never provided?
* A tendency to stay in relationships longer than I should, or to leave relationships without sufficient inquiry?

Ultimately, when we are in conflict with others, we have to choose whether to keep working on the relationship as is, or change the relationship status or the logistics. Might this relationship work if we decided to spend less time together, go on fewer trips together, or live in separate homes? The romance myth overvalues longevity and physical proximity in relationships, and makes it hard to sort through both our residual hopes from the initial courting period and our negative projections in the conflict phase. Both sets of projections tend to be overstated and ungrounded—our lover is neither the perfect angel we first perceived or the ungenerous grump we see in our worst moments. Even taking time to ask ourselves about the projections can help—you might use the What Else Is True? worksheet on p.48.

When we are considering breakup, it is useful to notice what *doesn't* support clear discernment. Don't seek advice from a dramatic friend who talks shit. Don't make decisions when you're hungry, tired, intoxicated, or hungover. Don't try to get help from your sibling who repeats romance-myth nonsense like "stay together no matter what." Perhaps most important, don't rely on the person you are considering breaking up with for direction. What would you add to this list of things not to do? How can you create a nonjudgmental, supportive space, either alone or with a confidant, to explore what to do?

Ultimately, no one can tell you when it is time to break up. With any conflict or difficulty, there are many paths forward, none of them certain. You might stay together and end up mired in resentment. You might decide to work through it and find growth and improved connection. You might wish you broke up sooner. You might break up and regret it. You might break up and find relief and better ways to access what you want.

The best we can hope for is to assess our current situations with as much care and kindness—and as little reactivity and autopilot script-following—as we can manage. Grief and loss are part of all relationships. Whatever decisions we make, we are forgoing the paths not taken. Trying to avoid experiencing any loss usually gets in the way of making thoughtful, sober decisions informed by our best insight.

When We Do Break Up

After two years together, Denise broke up with Kila. The two were fighting a lot. They had agreed to be in an open relationship, but Kila was very upset when Denise went on other dates, and often exploded in big outbursts, saying hurtful things. A few times Kila broke objects that mattered to Denise, and once Kila violated Denise's privacy by looking through her phone. Denise felt more and more avoidant of Kila and the outbursts, and sometimes downplayed or lied about her other lovers.

By the time they broke up, they were both hurt and upset. Kila still texts Denise with accusations and

Denise struggles not to respond and defend herself. Kila has been telling people in their circles about Denise's dishonesty, and some of Denise's friends and acquaintances are giving her the cold shoulder and not inviting her to events.

We break up with lovers, and also with collaborators, friends, and groups. When we break up with someone who does not want to be broken up with, we might fear we are being mean, that we are being unfair, that we are giving up too soon, or that they will punish or exclude us. When we get broken up with, we can feel abandoned and devastated, even if we did not enjoy the relationship much or were contemplating breakup ourselves—this is because rejection has its own meaning and impact. When we get to the point of breaking up, we're dealing with strong feelings from the conflict, in addition to the heightened feelings of the breakup itself. When we are going through such tumult, it's time to look out for distorted feelings and projections, to tread with care so that we can act according to our principles, as much as possible, and learn from our experiences.

Breaking up is okay to do. Deciding not to be in a particular kind of relationship with someone—to stop being lovers, roommates, co-stewarding a project, whatever you are breaking up from—is acceptable and part of being in relationships. We believe in consent. That means we all get to decide to leave particular activities, arrangements, and statuses. The other person does not have to agree to the breakup for it to be okay. People spend enormous amounts of energy trying to convince each other of their perspectives during breakups. The truth is, if you are breaking up, it's likely you disagree about some significant things, and whether to stay together may be one.

Sometimes, if we are the one breaking up, we want to get the other person's agreement in order to assuage our guilt. Sometimes, if we are being broken up with, we believe that if we can just get them to talk one more time, we can change their mind or make them see something about their behavior. These conversations often create more chances for hurt. When we reach the point of breaking up, there won't be agreement or compromise the way there might have been before we came to this point.

People break up to end a dynamic that isn't working for them, but it won't automatically end right away. If jealousy was a factor in the conflict, it also may continue after the breakup. The process of getting out of tangled dynamics is not quick or easy. We do some of the worst damage to each other and friends and community during breakup processes, or after breakup. When people are hoping to stay together, they might work harder to have compassion for the other person's perspective or actions. Once people separate, stored-up feelings of resentment, blame, judgment, and betrayal often come loose. We may also feel sadness from other wounds or losses from our pasts.

This is a time to handle ourselves with care, use emotional awareness tools, and seek support from trusted people. The person we are separating from is unlikely to be the right source of that support.

For those of us supporting a person through a breakup, it is also important to cultivate our own emotional awareness. When someone close to you is upset, what happens for you? Some of us learned unhelpful things in our families about ways of handling this, like shutting down, getting upset alongside them, joining their heightened state, or piling on blame and judgment for whoever they are upset with. We might feel uncomfortable around other people's strong feelings and be dismissive, or give unsolicited advice aimed at changing how they feel. When we are upset, most of us need to be listened to, to feel that someone is caring about our experience, and we may need specific support like a hug, company on a walk, time alone, some food, or whatever is most comforting. It is important not to assume that you know what will help, and to ask consent when making offers of supportive actions.

For people involved in a breakup, and anyone supporting them, it is vital to remember that gossip and campaigning can be very destructive. *Campaigning* is when we set out to get others to think poorly of the person we're mad at. When we are upset with someone, we may try to get others to show loyalty by excluding them. We might try to get our friends to help build a public case against that person.

This kind of campaigning after breakups often wreaks havoc on friend circles and communities working on political resistance, especially when people make accusations out of context. Vengefulness is likely to surface during breakups, when our feelings are stronger than usual. It's a good time to ask friends not only for comfort and care but also for help sticking to our principles. Sometimes, even years after a breakup, those strong feelings linger and are used to justify campaigning against someone. The more we can carefully attend to ourselves, notice reactivity, seek support, take the space we need from the other person, and choose principled action in the breakup period, the more we might prevent wide-rippling effects.

Even after you've broken up, it can be hard to stop seeing each other through the projections that went with the relationship. These projections fall into the two categories we discussed earlier in this chapter: the positive projections of wish fulfillment ("you are going to be the one who really loves me the way I want") and the negative projections of the conflict phase ("I am destroyed because you disappointed me and didn't deliver on what I hoped for"). We may experience either or both of these kinds of projections, with lots of urgent and inflated feelings, during breakup. For relationships involving kink, BDSM, Daddy or Mommy play, or other kinds of power exchange, breakups can be particularly charged. These dynamics intentionally engage with intense surrender and reenactment of childhood dynamics in ways that can be pleasurable and even healing. But relationships that generate heightened feelings and play off of childhood attachment wounds can make for tough separations.

Breaking up requires we move out of that category of heightened feeling toward each other that fueled the conflict. For lovers or partners, this might mean moving into the friend zone or becoming acquaintances. For best friends or roommates or collaborators, it means letting go of whatever was heightened in that relationship that made it hurt so bad. It can be hard when this relates to identities or experiences— "he understands what it's like to live with chronic pain" or "she was my only friend who is also an adoptee" or "they were my closest trans friend."

Many people try to skip this transition, hoping they can just break up, end the conflict and resume uninterrupted connection. If that doesn't work, which is often the case, periods of noncommunication can help, where you break some of the threads of the connection, feel the grief and loss of those dashed hopes, rely on other people for support or stimulation, and return to the relationship later to find out what is possible post-breakup. For some people, it is not until a lover starts a new relationship (or one that is particularly serious or public), or a best friend gets a new best friend, that they truly feel the loss and let go of the dynamic. These signals sometimes let us finally grieve and then, eventually, reconnect in a new way—if everyone wants to. We may wish it were not necessary to take time apart or halt communication, but more often than not, it is. Trying to skip it can lead to more heightened reactions and hurtful behavior.

There is no recipe for how best to break these dynamics, and there are no guarantees that people will want to be in each other's lives again. But the remedy of time apart can be immensely helpful. Making or meeting the kinds of demands that were common before breakup, trying to control one another's sex lives, being dishonest, or demanding inappropriate information are clues that the dynamics persist. These kinds of behavior indicate that people are in heightened emotional states, projecting on each other, and they can cause ongoing damage.

Taking a break from communication can stop these dynamics. If it is essential to communicate in dealing with logistics—about caring for children, pets, elders, finances, etc.—focus on defining the specific types of communication that are necessary, and how to limit it to those logistics rather than including other content from earlier dynamics. A trusted friend or therapist can help sort through communication boundaries in kind ways when we can't see the situation clearly.

Things to avoid when we are going through a breakup:

* Trying to convince someone to agree to a breakup
* Trying to persuade your lover not to break up with you

* Gossiping and campaigning
* Making controlling demands that are not appropriate or consensual
* Sabotaging shared projects or social spaces
* Cultivating or acting on vengeful feelings
* Not limiting contact enough to let grief happen

Things to look out for when supporting a friend who is going through a breakup:

* Shutting down emotionally when our friend is upset because it's hard to be present with their strong feelings
* Giving advice or being dismissive to try to halt someone else's strong feelings
* Joining or amplifying the strong feelings
* Gossiping and campaigning
* Supporting vengefulness

Breakups are among the times when we are most likely to abandon our principles, cause harm to others, and sow chaos and discord in our friend circles and communities. How many important projects that our communities really needed have been destroyed by people going off the rails after a breakup? We need each other badly now, and will even more as things intensify. We must learn to cultivate emotional awareness, ask for care and support, and try our best not to act our worst.

At a Jewish wedding many years ago, I was moved when the people getting married read from their ketubah, a Jewish marriage contract witnessed by the community during the ritual. In their ketubah, they agreed, in front of their loved ones, to act with compassion and integrity in the event that they decided to end the marriage for any reason. Rather than a fantasy wedding focused only on "happily ever after," they asked their community to witness their promises to care for each other in the event that they separate. This is truly loving: to know that conflict is inherent to relationships, to know that ending or changing a relationship is always a possibility. It implies that we should only stay if we want to, and should commit to be compassionate and kind even when we feel anger, jealousy, betrayal, and grief.

The romance cycle generates some of the strongest feelings people have in their lives, both pleasurable and painful. When we build up individuals or groups with positive projections, we inevitably experience disappointment as we get to know how fallible, inconsistent, and imperfect everyone is. Anticipating these cycles, and knowing that our feelings reflect societal patterns rather than reality, can help us ride the roller coaster without resorting to harmful actions. As we move from this chapter to explore common types of patterned conflicts and tools for navigating them in the next, it might be useful to reflect on prior experiences of breakups (yours or others'), and what you hope could happen next time.

* Did any of the difficulties described above emerge in breakups you've experienced? What did you learn about things to try next time?

* Did you get effective support during past breakups? What kinds of support would you like to have in place for your next breakup or loss?

* How do you respond when others are having strong feelings around you? Are there any skills you would like to sharpen in order to be more practiced at offering comfort and reducing harm to others?

* How do disposability culture, the romance myth, and scarcity mentality show up in breakups?

* What principles would you like to maintain or aspire to when ending relationships?

The next chapter, which investigates how the fears of abandonment and engulfment we may have developed in childhood play out in our adult relationships, looks into these patterns of conflict and suggests pathways out of them.

Chapter Three Recap:

* We may be drawn to and choose people who, because of their actual traits or traits we are perceiving or projecting, remind us of how we felt with our childhood caregivers.

* The stronger the attraction, the more intense our projections are. We unconsciously believe we will finally get the love we did not get from our caregivers. We may unconsciously feel we need this person or relationship to survive.

* We are attracted to people who have traits and emotional capacities that we unconsciously decided, early in our lives, we had to cut out of ourselves in order to survive. Those same traits become annoying or threatening after the early romance phase.

* Breakups can stir our most reactive feelings. When we are breaking up, we need to get support to avoid gossip, campaigning, and vengeance, all of which harm our communities.

* Transitioning to a new kind of relationship, such as moving from lovers to friends, requires time for grief and to move out of the heightened feelings of the conflict stage. Most people need at least a phase of separation, where you cut back on some activities and communication.

Encountering Fear, and
the Courage to Say Yes and No

All companionship can consist only in the strengthening
of two neighboring solitudes. . . . for when a person
abandons himself, he is no longer anything, and when
two people both give themselves up in order to come
close to each other, there is no longer any ground beneath
them and their being together is a continual falling.
—RAINIER MARIA RILKE, letter to Paula Modersohn-
Becker, April 29, 1904

No one guided me to myself. I am the guide.
—MAHMOUD DARWISH, "A Rhyme for the Odes" (2003)

IN OUR RELATIONSHIPS we are both our unique selves and
a collection of practiced thoughts, feelings and behaviors we
learned from cultural and childhood conditioning. In this
chapter, we'll explore a common dynamic resulting from how
our wounds match up with others', in which one person is
caught up in a fear of engulfment while the other is caught up
by a fear of abandonment. Anyone can feel either, but there
are frequently patterns within a relationship—or, for some

people, across many of their relationships—where one of these fears is more prevalent. These fears can generate dynamics in which one person becomes "the demanding one" and the other "the withdrawing one."

Understanding these opposing and complementary fears in all types of relationships can help us become more aware of, and eventually break free from, the behaviors they script for us. Those scripts make it hard for us to identify what we want, to ask for it, to say no to what we don't want, and to respect other people saying no. We will look at how cultivating boundaries can prevent or resolve resentments and how this can help us develop a sense of choice and consent in our lives.

Fears of Abandonment and Engulfment

Marco has the same dating problems again and again. He gets attached fast and comes on strong. He messages people too much. He feels easily hurt if someone changes plans or doesn't want to spend as much time together as he does. He quickly wants to know where the relationship is going and if it's "serious." He is attracted to people who are a bit aloof, and he can tell that sometimes he scares them off with his enthusiasm. He just gets so excited, often giving gifts and proposing plans quickly.

Mickey finds it hard to date. Most people aren't appealing to Mickey, and attraction wears off fast when people start to annoy or crowd them. Even during times when they have put more effort into seeking out sex partners or finding someone to date, it never works out. They lose interest, especially after the other person starts to get all gooey or tries to label the relationship. They want a more active sex and dating life, and even potentially a long-term lover, but they aren't finding matches.

Fran feels like she is on a roller coaster when she's dating. Although she dates a lot, sometimes the slightest thing—a date rescheduling or someone declining an invitation—leaves her feeling devastated and forlorn. But then sometimes getting a little too much attention from a date, even someone she's into, makes her want to run screaming. It doesn't make sense, and she can't tell why she feels alternately so hot or cold.

Two of the key fears we experience in relationships of all kinds, but perhaps especially in romantic relationships, are fear of abandonment and fear of engulfment. In many relationships, it can feel like one person is acting more as the pursuer and the other as the distancer. Some people notice that they are consistently in one of those roles. Others notice that their role shifts depending on the relationship or even within the course of a relationship. These complementary fears can create a feedback loop, with each person's reactions getting more exaggerated in response to the other's. Being stuck in these roles can be frustrating, prevent connection, and cause conflicts to escalate or stagnate.

Before continuing, I want to suggest that we avoid labeling ourselves as one of the two types exclusively. Many self-help books encourage establishing ourselves as one type or another, often by taking a quiz and getting a score. Examining entrenched patterns is vital for building self-awareness, but we miss a lot if we only focus on how we play one role, disregarding times and contexts in which we might be on the other side. In fact, it can obscure self-inquiry to get too attached to believing we only play a particular role. For example, I have known people who are very aware of being caregivers in many relationships, but don't notice that they also receive care. I have also known people who view themselves as the incompetent, needy one, and therefore didn't notice that in some relationships and spaces they were the one who took charge and solved problems. Noticing our multiple tendencies can help us be more aware of what is actually happening, and help us move toward making conscious choices.

In general, fear of being abandoned makes us act clingy, possessive, and critical. Fear of being engulfed and losing oneself often makes us run away, distance ourselves, or withhold connection;[1] and sometimes this also includes criticism of the other's "neediness." The person fearing abandonment and the person fearing engulfment tend to blame each other for their own reactions. We might not even know we are experiencing fear, we just think "she's so flaky" or "he's too demanding" or make other judgments. We might also blame ourselves, like "if I weren't so needy he'd probably want to hang out more" or "if I were a better boyfriend, he wouldn't feel so insecure." Blaming other people for our feelings, or believing other people's feelings are our fault, leads to loads of trouble. Fears of abandonment and engulfment run deep, stemming from childhood wounds, and cause reactions that are often unconscious. Keeping this in mind can help us learn not to take others' fears personally. Rather than slinging arrows, we can recognize that fear is present and meet it with compassion.

These two fears can lead to accusations of actual abandonment or engulfment. However, unlike experiences in childhood where a caregivers' abandonment was an existential threat, with rare exceptions a partner leaving does not have life-or-death consequences. Adults who are being crowded have many options, including leaving the setting, the city, or the relationship. Bottom line: these fears *feel* life-threatening now because engulfment or abandonment in childhood was an overwhelming, life-threatening experience. However, to paraphrase psychotherapist David Richo, adults cannot be abandoned, only left. Adults cannot be engulfed, only crowded.[2]

These are feelings of abandonment or engulfment, not facts, especially if we have, or can create, other relationships for emotional and material support. Discovering the powerful reality that we are in the grips of a fear—but that the threat is only in our imagination and we are not actually at risk—can free us to have more choice and compassion.

Richo provides a chart about the ways that fear of abandonment and fear of engulfment can manifest. Some of the statements may sound too strong or not relevant to some readers, even if we recognize ourselves in some entries in this chart. I recommend you read through and notice if anything feels familiar, and gently inquire about any of the statements that generate a reaction in you.

Fear of Abandonment Fear of Independence so that one:	Fear of Engulfment Fear of dependency so that one:
Has trouble letting go when the other needs space	Has trouble making a commitment
Seeks maximum contact (clings)	Seeks more space (distances)
Is enmeshed or obsessive about the other's story	Takes the other for granted or is indifferent
Is caretaking of the other and not of oneself	Feels entitled to need fulfillment by the other
Always wants to give more (sense of never giving enough)	Construes giving as obligating or receiving as smothering
Goes along with others' ideas, plans, or timing	Needs to be in control, to make decisions, or to be right
Has no personal boundaries or bottom line for abuse	Has no tolerance of disloyalty or inadequacy

Accommodates or copes with any conduct	Has rigid boundaries with no tolerance of error
Is addicted to the other	Seduces the other and then withholds
Needs constant reassurance that the other will stay	Needs the other to "stay put while I come and go at will"
Fears aloneness	Becomes anxious with the extended togetherness
Rationalizes (makes excuses that enable coping)	Intellectualizes (thinks or explains away feelings)
Protects the other from the impact of one's own feelings	Avoids or minimizes one's own and the other's feelings
Shows fear, represses anger	Shows anger, represses fear
Distress in comings and goings	Distress in giving/receiving
Manifests clinging, closeness, and reaching out	Manifests coldness, rigidity and distance

* What entries on this chart feel familiar? Have you been in relationships where you mostly felt one or the other of these sets of fears? A mix?

* Have you ever noticed yourself blaming someone else for your fear of abandonment or engulfment? Have you ever blamed yourself for someone else feeling these things?

* What does it feel like to hear the idea that adults can neither be abandoned or engulfed?

Staying Connected, Even When We're Afraid

When Marco and Mickey first got together, their differences didn't feel like a problem. If Mickey was slow to text back and Marco shared that it made him insecure, Mickey would apologize and try to do better. They were both excited about the relationship and generous with each other, as Mickey learned to be a bit more present and attentive, while Marco learned to give Mickey space. However, now that the bliss of their initial incinerating sexual and intellectual connection has settled down a bit, their differences are causing more difficulties. When Mickey wants more time alone, Marco fears that Mickey has fallen out of love, is upset. Mickey feels that no matter how they show interest in Marco, it is never enough. Mickey feels guilty asking for space or saying no to Marco's invitations, and sometimes they say yes to plans but end up feeling resentful and acting distant. They are starting to feel smothered by Marco, exhausted with his insecurity, and hopeless about ever convincing Marco of their love.

Sometimes we unconsciously choose relationships because they stir up our fears. However, often instead of working through the fear, we go deeper into it, blaming the other person by creating a narrative in which the problem is not our fear but the other person's behavior. Not all relationships stir up these fears equally. Sometimes we choose a relationship where the fears are less intense and we get the chance to investigate them, because they are not stimulated to heights that throw us into reactivity and blame. Sometimes people dodge relationships that stir up any fears at all in order to avoid this, which might mean the relationship is less intense.[3] We can cultivate awareness about this, asking ourselves if our fears are limiting our potential growth, or if the choice to pursue a less reactive relationship is a useful space for learning.

These fears usually emerge after the euphoric "honeymoon" period described in the previous chapter is over. For some people, the fears also create "negative excitement," including an adrenaline rush. Some people unconsciously provoke behavior in others that will stimulate these fears and provide this rush.[4] Even "negative" feelings can be familiar, comforting, or stimulating in ways that make our lives feel "real" because they unconsciously remind us of formative relationships with our caregivers. It may feel both bad and compelling because it is such a well-worn groove. I have known people from families where caregivers gave "the silent treatment," who later unconsciously sought out partners who used that tactic in arguments. It might feel terrible because it was done to us as kids, but simultaneously feel familiar, compelling, even irresistible.

One useful experiment we can try when we notice any fixed roles emerging in our relationships is to switch roles in ordinary, practical activities: if one person plans dates, makes decisions, drives, cooks, cleans, goes out, stays home, initiates important conversations, or initiates touch, see what it feels like for the other person to do this, instead. It is hard to change emotional styles or fear patterns, but we can often switch daily activities that may be manifestations of stagnated dynamics. This exercise works for people in romantic relationships, friendships, and collaborations of all kinds. If one person always organizes the food, or takes the notes, or stays last to clean and lock up, or pays attention to who is feeling left out, or remembers birthdays, it can be beneficial to intentionally have someone else try that role or activity.

In the process, we can expand our range, build skills, and reflect on what emotional settings might lead to repeated roles and tasks. Our accustomed roles can be gratifying or comfortable, chosen because we like them or feel good at them. But they can also be exhausting or form resentments when we feel forced to perform them because no one else will. People often feel resentment when their labor is assumed rather than requested and recognized.

* Can you think of patterned roles you take on during ordinary activities with dates, friends, coworkers, family members, or housemates?
* Are there any places where you hold resentments, feeling like you "always have to" or "never get to" do something?
* Could you intentionally switch roles for some of the activities listed? What would it take?

Attachment Styles, Core Fears, and Conflict

ALONGSIDE FEARS OF abandonment and engulfment, patterns of reactivity cause some people to make demands while others withdraw. The idea of "anxious" or "avoidant" (or "secure") attachment style is popular in self-help literature and memes these days, especially in the form of internet quizzes to determine your attachment style. As I mentioned above, the results of any personality tests focused on distinct categories should be taken with a grain of salt. Nonetheless, the idea is that we learn fundamental things about how to be safely emotionally attached to others in early childhood. Those lessons show up in our adult relationships in anxious–avoidant dynamics. This approach to thinking about our connections is a useful part of our efforts to free ourselves from autopilot.

Human beings crave and need secure attachment. We need to feel that others are accessible, responsive, and engaging. We want to know from people we love: Can I reach you? Can I rely on you to respond to me emotionally? Do I know that you will value me and stay close?[5] Secure connection with others makes it possible to be flexible, curious, and open. Much conflict originates from acting out of the fear and panic of insecurity. Statistics show that relationship stress increases heart and blood pressure problems and decreases immunity.[6] The stress people suffer from relationship dynamics is very real and can make us miserable and sick. This is true of romantic relationships, and also of stressful relationships with work, family, groups, and friends.

Codependence and Interdependence

The popular term *codependence*, used as a way of describing sticky relational dynamics, can seem to imply that we are or should be independent individuals—that dependency on each other is dysfunctional. An attachment-centered approach to relationships lets go of that illusion. Capitalism, white supremacy, and ableism moralize and glorify the idea of autonomous individuality, but liberation movements combat this idea, arguing that we are all interconnected with and *inter*dependent on each other and the planet. Denying our need for each other devalues both care labor, typically done by women and people of color, and people who are cast as "dependent," often people with disabilities, poor people, old people, and children.

In reality, everyone survives through others' care. An attachment approach embraces the fact that we have deep needs for emotional security in relationships with other people. At the same time, if we define codependence as the tendency to blame others for our feelings or take responsibility for other people's feelings, without buying into false notions of "independence," it can be a useful framework. See Chapter Six for more exploration of codependent dynamics.

The Seattle Public Library

Columbia Branch

www.spl.org

Checked Out On: 4/26/2025 16:29
XXXXXXXXX8336

Item Title	Due Date
0010109951680	5/10/2025

Love in a f*cked-up world : how to build
relationships, hook up, and raise hell
together

# of Items: 1

Renew items at www.spl.org/MyAccount
or 206-386-4190
Sign up for due date reminders
at www.spl.org/notifications

Download the SPL app!
Get the app to search our catalog and
borrow books from your Apple or Android
device.
www.spl.org/App

Maybe you have noticed strong physical sensations that come during conflict and signal panic, such as shaking, getting cold, feeling light-headed, sweating, or experiencing stomach pain. How easily we can be thrown into that heightened state depends on how emotionally secure we feel overall in our lives. The panic can be activated by real or imagined threats.[8] It can be stirred up if the other person was late or did not call back, said no to sex, asked for sex, chose to spend time with someone else, mentioned that they were disappointed in a plan that fell through, made a request of us that we wanted to say no to, or any number of other things. Most of us can easily think of objectively harmless behaviors by others that have provoked a fear of abandonment or engulfment in us at one time or another. Romantic relationships are particularly likely to provoke these fears. However, this kind of panic also occurs in other relationships. I consistently see it in conflicts within social movement groups.

Once we experience this panic, either we become demanding and clinging (anxious attachment)—trying to draw comfort and reassurance from our lover, friend, coworker, or family member—or we withdraw and detach to soothe and protect ourselves (avoidant attachment). The demanding and clinging approach is something like "Notice me! Be with me, I need you." The withdrawing response is something like "I won't let you hurt me. I will chill out and try to stay in control."[9] Both responses are an expression of insecurity and fear.

We often enter cycles of increasing activation in a pattern of mutual insecurity. The one in the demanding role tries harder and harder to get the other person to respond, while the one in the withdrawing role withdraws more and more. For the demanding one, provoking the withdrawing person can include provoking negative attention.[10] For kids, when getting positive attention is not possible, negative attention can feel like the next best thing, better than being ignored, because it offers some form of connecting.

People experiencing the demanding side of the dynamic, where they feel highly critical of the other person and might be fearing abandonment, say and think things like:[11]

* "She doesn't care that I am in so much pain about this."
* "He acts like my feelings are made up and baseless and I should just shut them down."
* "I feel like she's not there for me, I can't find her, we're never really together and connected."
* "I feel so alone in this relationship. I can't bear it."
* "They are so distant when I am in pain and need them."
* "I get so mad at their nonresponsiveness. No matter how loud I scream, they just sit there."
* "I feel like if I never said anything about what is going on, we would just grow apart, our relationship would be empty, and he wouldn't even care."

Those experiencing the withdrawing side of the dynamic, who fear being engulfed by the other person, may think or say things like:

* "I can't do anything right with him. He makes me feel totally inadequate."
* "I just feel numb when I hear this criticism. I don't have anything to say."
* "When this conversation starts I space out, go into another world. Can't respond."
* "I feel overwhelmed when I hear this stuff and I freeze and go silent."
* "I get really calm when this starts, waiting for her to calm down, waiting for this to be over."
* "I don't feel like I matter. All I am is this person who is doing this set of things he wants, either well or badly, he is the judge, I wait to be judged."
* "I get logical, try to offer solutions and advice, but that just makes them angrier at me, it seems."
* "They're just too needy and clingy. I'm not like that, I'm independent."
* "The relationship is fine. I don't know why they make up this idea of a crisis."

The withdrawing person may also experience withdrawal as loss of interest in the relationship, or feelings of avoidance, like not wanting to call the person back, touch, or hang out.

Anxious and avoidant dynamics sometimes manifest as a fight in which one person is arguing that something is wrong while the other is arguing that things are fine. Sometimes both people feel like something is wrong, but they disagree about what it is exactly that's causing the issue. A common feature is that, again and again, they end up in the same conflict, playing the same roles, and feel stuck.

* Can you recall times when you have gone into a demanding or withdrawing reaction?
* Are there certain types of relationships where you are more likely to react with insecure demands or insecure withdrawal?
* Are there relationships where you and the other person switch back and forth between these roles?

Neglectful and Intervening Caregivers History Inquiry

These questions can help understand our caregiver histories, surface hidden patterns, find compassion for ourselves, and make more conscious choices when fears come up.

* Of your childhood caregivers, were some controlling or overintervening? (e.g., little privacy; less choice about

eating, clothing, or hygiene; pressure and scrutiny of your activities; physical invasiveness).

* If so, how did you cope? (e.g., kept things secret, gave up your own interests for those your caregiver pushed, withdrew, tried to appease).

* As an adult, have you been drawn to people who are intrusive or intervening? Or have you been hypervigilant for people being intrusive, sensitive to any inkling of being controlled, even when your concern was unwarranted?

* Of your childhood caregivers, were some neglectful? (e.g., failing to provide structure; disinterested in your needs; unavailable due to work, substance use, mental health, illness, or physical distance).

* If so, how did you cope? (e.g., found other adults' attention, withdrew and became overly self-sufficient, attempted to attain that caregiver's attention, provoked negative attention by misbehaving)

* As an adult, have you been drawn to people who are aloof or give you their attention inconsistently? Or have you ever been hypervigilant of people withdrawing their attention or leaving you, even if it wasn't happening? Have you ever felt insatiable for others' attention? Or have you done things that you wish you hadn't to get or keep others' attention?

Boundaries

THE DYNAMICS CREATED by our fears of abandonment and engulfment make it hard to ask for what we want, to say no to one another, or accept another person's no. "Boundaries" is one of those catchphrases that—despite its overuse in the self-help canon—is actually quite important. Learning how to authentically say yes and no to others requires understanding our histories of shutting off feelings, acting against our well-being, suppressing desires and needs, and feeling ashamed, in order to survive our early lives. To get by in our families, schools, and other formative experiences, most of us have sometimes coped by shutting down or numbing. As a result, sometimes we don't know what we want and don't want, what we feel or believe. This can make us struggle to authentically say yes or no to others, and to accept that others will say yes and no to us. If we want to be people who can align our actions with our values, we need to break out of autopilot reactions and build these boundary-making and boundary-respecting skills.

For many of us, after a lifetime of punishment, humiliation, rejection, or shame, it is difficult to believe that we are allowed to be authentic about our wants. We can have an automatic "no" or "yes" setting, or different auto-responses that come up in particular contexts. For example, some people might have an automatic "no" when they are invited to move their bodies where others can see. They may have desires to swim, sing, dance, box, jump rope, or something else, but they decline to explore them. Others may have an automatic "yes" to requests for social time, but a suppressed or unconscious desire for solitude, reflection, or solo pursuits. Many people have an auto-response to sex or touch, which gets in the way of chances to explore our authentic desires.

We also have strong responses to other people's "yes" and "no." Some of us were trained through parenting and cultural norms to submit to others' wills. Some of us learned to aggressively push for dominance. These strong tendencies may show up differently in different settings: many of us might have had a caregiver who was dominating at home but submissive to authority at work or vice versa.

When we first learn about boundaries, we might unconsciously swing to the extreme pole. It can be ungraceful, but that overcorrection makes sense as we struggle toward brand-new practices, flexing muscles that have not yet been trained for nuance. It's important to be patient with ourselves and our friends and lovers during these bumpy moments of growth and experimentation. Boundaries often fall away most easily at the beginning of the romance cycle, when people are starry-eyed and lost in heady emotions and positive projections. Boundaries sometimes become rigid in periods of conflict.

Some signs that your boundaries need strengthening are when you:[12]

* Are unsure about your preferences
* Don't notice or assess your satisfaction in a relationship, just try to keep it going
* Walk on eggshells around the other people, shaping yourself to others' moods or needs
* Don't know your own truth, instead taking whatever the other person said as true
* Deprioritize care for yourself, meeting others' needs instead
* Tolerate actions from other people that you'd advise a friend not to accept
* See another person as your source of happiness, enjoyment, creativity, or excitement
* Have difficulty feeling anger
* Can't say no, do too much for others

* What entries on this list stand out?
* Are there relationships where you frequently fail to respect your own preferences or limits, share them with others, ask others to respect them?
* Are there times or situations in which you have seen yourself become overly rigid about your preferences and inflexible in demanding others adhere to them? What causes that and what does it feel like?

Boundary-Making Can Be a Way to Re-Parent Ourselves

When Les was a kid, their parents worked a lot, so they and their siblings came home, ate, did homework, played, and went to bed with little supervision. Les enjoyed this freedom and autonomy, but as an adult, they have a hard time putting themselves to sleep, and they eat erratically. This causes them to be irritable and impatient, and to struggle to concentrate when they need to. It took their best friend pointing this out for them to realize that their eating and sleeping habits were a big obstacle to feeling the way they want.

Learning to strengthen our boundaries could be understood as learning to parent ourselves. Many of us come to adulthood struggling to respect both our own needs, feelings, and desires and those of others. Ideal parenting would help kids feel secure *and* free to develop autonomy, however, many parents are either overbearing or neglectful. Ideal parenting would provide structure and routine, but also model flexibility and negotiation. However, many parents either enforce overly rigid structure or don't provide sufficient consistency. Ideal parents would model balancing taking care of themselves with the needs of their kids and jobs, but many of us were raised by people who were numb, addicted, traumatized, depressed, martyred, or self-centered, and consequently, were parenting under conditions that make this balance impossible. As adults, we can learn to provide ourselves with what was missing in the parenting we got. This can be as simple as giving ourselves a bedtime or routines for eating. We may also need to change negative childhood messages to self-talk that supports our well-being, for example changing "You lazy piece of shit, get up!" to "If it sounds fun to go outside, let's do it! A breath of air sounds nice."

Cristien Storm, author of *Empowered Boundaries: Speaking Truth, Setting Boundaries, and Inspiring Social Change*, writes:

> When we use boundaries to try to avoid fear and anxiety, we deny ourselves opportunities to learn how to handle these emotions in healthier ways.... For example, we don't set boundaries with our supervisor, so we set them with our partner because it feels safer; we say no to a desired relationship because it feels too scary to face the feelings that come up... There are times when we need to set [firm] boundaries. We don't worry about whether we are avoiding or letting ourselves feel fear when we yank a child out of the way of a speeding bus. The problem is when avoiding emotions becomes an automatic response across situations.[13]

Most of us have a combination of overly rigid boundaries and missing boundaries. We might feel like a doormat with our family of origin but be a taskmaster with our roommates, or the reverse. We might be suppressing anger but find ourselves often stuck in dread and sadness. Stepping into our integrity in our relationships and in our lives inevitably includes looking at which boundaries we have in place and which are missing, and making intentional adjustments.

Fear, Distorted Motivations, and Loss of Boundaries in Romance

Tex met Lou six months ago and fell fast and hard. Tex is an appeaser; she has a hard time saying no to people. Lou has a big personality, is very charismatic, and really goes for what they want. Tex was swept up, and made a lot of changes in her life quickly, including moving to another state with Lou, and quitting two important projects she was involved in. Her friends have tried to raise concerns with her about it but have noticed that she stops responding to anyone who brings it up.

The dynamics we've been looking at, so far—the romance myth, scarcity mentality and disposability, fear of abandonment or engulfment, struggles with boundaries—can, when combined, become a dangerous cocktail in our lives, one that creates painful and damaging relationship conflict. The results can look like all kinds of common sketchy behavior, some of which I listed on p. 115.

These behaviors can be disruptive in small or large ways. They can lead to increased isolation in relationships and can cause hurt or harm. Isolation undermines our safety. Who will help us when we get sick or have a crisis? Who can help us sort out difficult situations or feelings? In groups and movements, these dynamics can cause:

* People being exiled from groups or projects
* The failure of important projects and collaborations
* Long-term bad blood being established, which divides people who need each other
* People leaving resistance work because of the toxicity
* Groups being vulnerable to law enforcement infiltration and disruption

These behaviors are so common that they are often minimized or taken for granted, or individualized. But these aren't our individual failings, they are cultural patterns that we need to unpack collectively, by changing our own behaviors and supporting others to do the same.

Understanding the root causes of these behaviors in ourselves and others is essential to our personal and our communities' well-being and to our fight for liberation. We must commit ourselves to finding new ways to manage the cultural baggage and strong feelings that pervade our relationships.

Real Talk About Relationships

WHAT DO BALANCED relationships, or relationships with less reactivity and more consent, look like? How would relationships feel that *do* support our well-being, the wellness of people around us, our liberation movements, and the planet? To build relationships like that, we have to understand that:[14]

* No one can control or change someone else, and it is not necessary to do so.

* Genuine intimacy requires constant permission to come closer or take more distance; we are always changing.

* No one can love and satisfy us perfectly; we are responsible for our own happiness.

* No one is perfectly honest all the time—feelings of betrayal are part of intimacy.

* We all show up with wounds that limit our abilities to connect, feel, communicate, and be intimate. The best we can do is to try to be aware of this and to be compassionate to ourselves and others.

* Blaming others and trying to be right undermines our healing and connection.

* We are naturally inclined toward healing and freedom, but we have a lot of baggage to work through with humility.

* Powerful attraction often tells us more about our own childhood shaping and settings than whether the other person is a good match for us.

These points are a sober antidote to the romance myth. For some of us, these points may feel harsh. Letting go of the romantic fantasy that someone will appear to make us happy can be challenging, and we may resist the reality that we cannot control other people or force them to stay with us. To me, it is a relief to realize that the kinds of struggles I have experienced internally and in relationships are the norm—most of us wrestle with intimacy, dishonesty, and intense feelings. I am not more fucked up or damaged than other people. Having a sincere desire to examine our motivations and reactions and align them with our values can help us learn to love well and be loved well. Of course, this is no small feat—it's a lifelong exploration.

The final point, about attraction, on the list above reminds us that we often actively fantasize, or can tap into cultural fantasies, that someone else (or some new job, new organization, new subculture, new exercise fad, new town) will make us whole and complete and happy. It can mean that when someone or something is attractive and stirs our childhood wounds, we quickly lose our principles, chalking it up to being struck by Cupid's arrow. We can cause great pain, loss, and conflict if we chase the mythical promise of novelty on autopilot, overcome by projections about the new person or thing. Instead, we need to balance our excitement about new attractions with accountability to existing connections, and work to sustain, change, or end them in a principled way.

Many of us might have a laundry list of complaints about our own experiences in relationships. Most of us also have plenty of criticisms of others' relationships. Few of us have clear criteria for what having supportive, loving connections to ourselves and others is actually like. The list below might help you think through how current relationships meet your expectations, and what boundary work is needed to bring them even more into alignment. This list, useful for all kinds of relationships, helps identify where we find greater ease or more difficulty, and what wounds that deserve our attention and compassion underlie those struggles.[15] See which of these you can answer yes to.

* I feel supported enough by myself and my friends that I am not desperately in need of someone to depend on or take care of.
* I trust myself to receive loyalty and handle betrayal if it comes. I know that people will change, levels of closeness will change, and none of us are strictly consistent.
* I am able to give and receive, even when it brings up fear.
* I respect others' ground rules about responsibilities, differing needs for space, time, sex; I also expect my ground rules and needs to be respected.
* I am encouraging and accepting of others' unique needs and differences. I don't have to be afraid or feel threatened when I encounter these differences.

* I am able to focus on others' feelings and concerns, listening carefully without the immediate need to tell my own story.

* I can sustain a commitment to relationships even if all my needs are not being met, since I value others for their inherent worth, not just for fulfilling my needs. I can also let go when a relationship is not good for me anymore.

* I can tolerate love and anger at the same time.

* I can get excited about new people, relationships, ideas, and projects, and still sustain interest and connection with those to whom I am committed. I need not act impulsively or urgently to enjoy the pleasures of excitement and novelty.

* Does reading these lists help you realize anything you want to grow or cultivate? Do any of these points generate feelings of relief? What about disappointment?

* Are some of the criteria in the second list already true for you in some of your relationships? Have you seen them in anyone else's lives?

* What concrete actions would help you get more of what you want?

Negative Self-Talk, Fear, and Anxiety

Negative self-talk comes in many forms. It can be self-assessments, "I'm ugly, I'm lazy, I can't sing, etc." It can be anxiously repeated questions, "Will I get the job?" "Does she like me?" It can be rigid (yet ungrounded and unkind) assertions, "I have to get this house clean by five." "I need to lose fifteen pounds." Becoming aware of these messages—and the patterns of feeling that generate them—can help us break free of them. The key to dealing with negative and fearful self-talk is understanding that we cannot ignore it, judge it, or believe it. Instead, we can take active steps to shift and change it. Journal or just spend time thinking about these prompts:

* When do I usually get anxious or afraid?
* What kinds of negative self-talk are coming up?
* How does fear/anxiety feel in my body?
* What do I do when fear or anxiety comes up? (e.g., push it down, find distractions, judge myself, follow fearful ideas and chew on them, get action-oriented and do a bunch of tasks)
* List three aspects of fear and/or anxiety that get in your way. Then write down what you want instead. You can focus on particular areas of your life: sex, activism, body image, living space, friendships, food, money, spirituality, relationship with nature, family, sleep, creativity.

* Spend five minutes (you could do this daily) imagining the "what you want" prompt above, universally or in just one area.
* Once a day, write down three anxious or fearful thoughts, and then write three positive or counterbalancing thoughts that are true. (The What Else Is True? worksheet on p. 48 can help.)
* Imagine yourself five minutes after the thing you are afraid of has passed, such as the job interview, the hard conversation, the exam, or whatever it is.

Yes? No? Maybe?

Shoshana's friend circle and queer subculture are very sex positive. People dress up, flirt, have raucous parties, write and talk about sex, and value promiscuity. It is thrilling and freeing for her, but it's also a bit outside her comfort zone. She wants to shed shame and restriction, but she is also secretly struggling with internalized norms from mainstream culture. She wants her friends to think she's edgy and cool. When she goes to sex parties with a new date who makes out with other people in front of her, Shoshana seethes with jealousy, but tries to hide it. She feels like she can't express what's happening, so she makes up reasons to withdraw, even from people she likes and is attracted to.

Do any of the narratives below feel familiar?

* "When people approach me with romantic or sexual invitations, I just go along with it. I'm not even sure what I want."

* "I know I'm overcommitted, but when someone asks me to do another big task, I just can't say no. I feel resentful, and want people to stop asking."

* "When people ask me to do social things, even though I know it would probably be good for me, it doesn't sound appealing, and I just automatically say no."

* "When people ask me to do things, I just say 'maybe,' knowing I will later slink out of doing it, or ghost if I don't feel like it."

* "As soon as someone approaches me with a request, I become hyperfocused on what they want to hear. It drowns out whether I want to say yes or no."

* "I've realized that I say 'no' more harshly than I intend. It's like I'm unsure if it is okay to say no, so I get defensive, and it can come out pretty mean."

* "I feel snubbed whenever my partners or friends say 'no' to my invitations. I know it's fine if they don't want to join me, but it feels like rejection, and I withdraw."

* "I don't ask people for things unless I know they will say 'yes.'"

* "I feel mad when my partner says 'no' when I want to hang out or have sex. Their rejection sets me off every time."

* "It's hard to ask for things, and even when I get up the
  nerve and someone says 'yes,' half the time I disappear.
  I don't feel like I deserve it, so I sabotage it."
* "I get impatient when people are making a decision
  about something I have asked. I can't handle waiting,
  not knowing if they'll say yes or not. Sometimes I can be
  a bit pressuring."

Consent is central to self-determination. Lack of consent is
what defines violence and abuse—like unwanted sexual touch,
unwanted medical intervention, unwanted surveillance, or
being displaced, locked up, or deported. Feminist resistance
movements taught me that we should get to choose what happens to us, and should be able to say no.

Most people I know want to give or withhold consent
freely, and also to be able to say "maybe" when they need time
to consider a request or learn more. We want to stop the violence and coercion that robs people of self-determination, of
their ability to consent and refuse consent. Obstacles to consent are both within and outside us. The outside ones are easier to spot: our collective action aims to change systems of
violence, and the individual people acting them out. However,
we also experience barriers to authentic consent *inside* us as
we cope with those systems. Very few of us are truly free to
answer requests in complete alignment with our wellbeing.
Rather, pressure and social conditioning lead to autopilot

answers, when we feel like we don't have options, or we find answering so stressful that we don't really know what we want.

As kids, we were punished for saying no—we had to do what adults told us to do at home and at school. We adopted a range of survival tactics: appeasing someone dominant, saying yes in the moment and hoping to find workarounds later, giving in and doing stuff we did not want to do, keeping others at a distance as much as possible, forcing our will on others, or saying maybe no matter what we really wanted. We also learned unconsciously from watching how our caregivers got by, and we may still be mimicking this behavior without even knowing it.

* What was a recent time when you said yes or no to something you wish you had answered the other way? What was that like? What did it feel like in your body?
* Is yes, no, or maybe an automatic default answer for you? In all situations or in particular situations? Which ones?
* For some people, when they say "maybe," they really feel or mean "no." For others, "maybe" really means "yes." Do you see yourself in either of these groups? What does *maybe* protect you from saying or feeling?

Authentic Yes/No/Maybe Calculator

Use this tool when someone asks you to do something and you want to make sure you answer authentically, rather than on autopilot.

☐ *Do I feel dread?*

☐ *How does my body feel when I think about the thing I am being asked? (Consider temperature, texture, skin sensations, what your guts feel like, whether you feel light or heavy, cloudy or clear, any pain, irritation, numbness, or tingling.)*

☐ *Am I delaying answering? If so, why?*

☐ *Am I afraid to ask for more time before answering? If so, what am I afraid of?*

☐ *Do I feel like I should say yes? Why?*

☐ *Do I have a story about what saying yes or no will mean about me?*

☐ *Am I being realistic about what this will be like?*

☐ *Am I being honest about how much time and energy this will take? What do I know from past experiences?*

☐ *Am I being honest about what interacting with these people/this person will be like? What do I know from past experience that can make this clearer?*

☐ *What will it take to recover from this?*

☐ *If I believed I am already okay exactly as I am and that whatever I want to do or not do is okay, what would I say to this request?*

☐ *Do I need more time to examine my feelings so I know whether I want to do this or not? Can I ask for more time?*

Respecting Others' Yes, No, and Maybe

Jozi and Mustafa have been together for three years and have sex very infrequently. Jozi feels rejected and wishes they had sex more often. Mustafa isn't sure why he is avoidant about affection, but it feels related to his intermittent depression, and the lack of alone time and space now that they are both working from home in their small apartment. He knows he should ask for some alone time in the apartment once in a while, but he is afraid Jozi will react negatively, so he doesn't bring it up. Sometimes when Jozi tries to initiate sex, and Mustafa doesn't feel like it, Jozi can be a bit verbally pressuring, first asking Mustafa to just try making out and see how it goes, and then, if he says no to that, getting upset and being critical of him and the relationship. Mustafa feels even more avoidant after these incidents.

Many of us who oppose sexual violence may feel like we value consent and honor others' consent. However, we could all learn more about the ways we respond to yes, no, and maybe. Many of us expect a "yes" from a lover, family member, best friend, or roommate regarding particular requests.

In intimate relationships, many people do more indirect maneuvering to get others to do what they want. It is uncomfortable to notice where we may not be authentically honoring the consent of others. We can commit to getting to a place where we all honor each other's self-determination. Here are some questions to help initiate this inquiry:

* When do I avoid asking directly for what I want because I don't want to get a "no"? (Think about friends, family, dates, coworkers, collaborators, acquaintances, authority figures, roommates.)

* What sensations come up when I think about someone saying "no" to me in one of those areas or relationships?

* Are there any indirect things I do to avoid getting the answer "no"? When? With which people?

* When did someone recently say "no" to me? What did it feel like? What were my physical sensations, emotions, and thoughts? How did I respond to the other person?

* How would I like to be when intaking others' responses to my requests? What can I cultivate in my relationships regarding yes, no, and maybe?

* What would change if my experience was more aligned with
  my values in this area of my life, or if I was more skilled in this?
* Are there any people in my life who might be scared to
  say "no" to me? How come? What is my part in that?

Charlie Glickman, a somatic sex therapist, has developed a useful tool for practicing consent and direct communication about desires. He recommends a simple formula. The first part is an "if" statement that acknowledges that the person may or may not have the time, energy, interest, or resources to do what you are asking. It lets them know that you are interested in whether they really want to and are able to say yes. The second part is a direct statement of what you want. Here are some examples:

* If you have time, I would like you to help me clean up the
  living room.
* If you are interested, I would like to go see a movie with
  you on Saturday.
* If you want, I would like to go to the party together.
* If you are up for it, I want you to rub my shoulders.
* If you have the energy, I would like you to finish the dishes.
* If you're interested, I want to make out with you.

This formula is different from how I learned to ask for things. I have always said, "Do you want to help me clean up the living room?" This phrasing lets me avoid claiming my own desire. It's as if I am not making a request for labor, but inviting someone to do something they want. In reality, I am requesting labor, and—even if they aren't burning with desire to clean—they still might be willing to help me out. When I started using Charlie's phrasing, it felt uncomfortable— having to ask directly meant admitting I wanted something. The phrasing I was using before has deep roots of shame and devaluing myself.

In *Empowered Boundaries*, Cristien Storm writes that "hinting or sideways communication stops us from learning how to sit with the fear and anxiety of asking for what it is we truly want." In the vignette above, we saw how Mustafa's fear of asking for the alone time he wants fuels his disinterest in sex and being affectionate with Jozi. We saw how Shoshana's shame about her feelings and wants led her to feel a sense of distance from the people she wanted to be connected with. Avoiding asking for what we want in some parts of a relationship can dull desire and interest in other parts. Anxiety about being direct might stem from how the other person has acted in the past, or what we learned in childhood about not asking for what we want. In either case, every time anxiety steers us to avoid direct communication, we strengthen that path in the relationship—and that link in our own minds—that connects our desires to anxiety/avoidance feelings.[16]

WHEN I BEGAN to practice Charlie's phrasing, people in my life responded positively. When you admit that you want something, the other person can feel it's possible to give a cleaner yes or no, rather than feeling like you are maneuvering to get them to do something. When you try on Charlie's phrasing, does it show you anything about how you tend to avoid direct requests? How does it feel to be more direct?

Consent is a framework for understanding everything we are trying to heal and change in ourselves and in the world. Our movements are fighting against governments and corporations controlling our lives, putting our people in cages, fighting endless wars for profit, and making the planet uninhabitable. We want everyone to get to decide for themselves how to live. If we are to collaborate to survive the disasters shaping our lives and to destroy systems of domination, we need to root out the programming that dominant culture has implanted in us.

It can be painful to observe how we are acting out scripts that don't match our values, and responding to people in our lives based on old wounds rather than our most loving intentions. The first step in this work is becoming more aware of our current patterns and practices, and being compassionate with ourselves about what we find. Then, we can begin to explore what new practices might be possible. The next chapter brings us deeper into what happens when we fight with each other, and how we can break out of and recover from stagnating conflicts.

Chapter Four Recap

* One of the most common patterns in relationships is a dynamic in which one person's fear of abandonment is activated, while the other person's fear of engulfment is activated.

* This dynamic can also be understood as one person being demanding while the other is distancing, or one person being anxious and the other is avoidant.

* These fears are powerful and can cause states of panic that escalate conflict.

* When we notice these fears are present, we can shift from blaming each other for our fears and into finding compassion for our own and each other's fears. We can stop taking it all personally and de-escalate the conflict.

* Fear can prevent us from knowing what we really want and asking for it in our relationships. It can also cause us to disrespect other people's preferences or limits.

* Learning how to identify what we want and don't want and communicate about it directly can help us heal the underlying wounds that generate these core fears.

What Are We Fighting About?:
Communication and Repair

All movement is a sign of thirst.
Most speaking really says
"I am hungry to know you."
—HAFIZ

Mustafa and Jozi always seem to be arguing about time. Jozi gets frustrated when Mustafa stays out later than he planned with his brothers, who play games together on Tuesdays. Jozi works early in the morning and misses sleep when Mustafa comes back late. Mustafa tries to get home on time, but his night with his brothers is the highlight of his week.

This seems like a basic logistics conflict, but these conversations tend to turn into fights that feel terrible, with Jozi feeling like Mustafa doesn't care about her sleep and work, and Mustafa feeling that Jozi doesn't see all that he does to accommodate her schedule.

FREQUENTLY IN OUR relationships, it seems as though we are fighting about dishes, punctuality, money, sex, or chores, when really what's *under* the surface is much more important. When we work to root out the fundamental fears that drive the conflict, we can move on to real transformation.

What we are really fighting for is this: to feel loved and secure, to feel seen and valued, to feel free to be ourselves. We all enter relationships with histories that color the roles we take in conflicts. The more we were cared for in a way that allowed us to feel safe, connected, and autonomous in our early lives, the easier it is to tolerate the differences that come up in our adult relationships. The less we got that kind of love, however, the more panicked our reactions can become during conflicts, and the more difficult it can be to recover. Sexual and romantic relationships are where many people experience some of their most heightened insecurity. This is why these relationships often become the source of such sharp conflicts, out-of-line behavior, and suffering.

In the last chapter, we looked at how fears of abandonment and engulfment shape our fights, how they cause us to take up demanding or withdrawing behaviors. Becoming aware of those patterns, rather than run by them, allows us to explore new ways to connect and get our emotional needs met.

Ideally, we can shift away from a resentful, criticism-driven focus. Rather than trying to be "right" in a fight, we can become responsive to our *own* needs, find our authentic yes and no, and respect other people's yes and no. We can move from reacting in ways that disconnect us from loved ones—criticism, withdrawal, tantrums—to focus on finding connection even in the face of hard-wired panic responses. As we discussed in Chapter Three, building self-awareness around these patterns can also include recognizing which signals tell us we need to leave a relationship.

Relationships aren't all good or all bad. They are made up of moments where we feel close or don't, get scared or don't, find comfort or don't. We can build skills to understand what is happening during conflict, learn to move past our autopilot reactions, and find ways to turn moments of discord into times of greater connection.

In this chapter, we'll look at *sore spots*—those particular topics, actions, and words that we each have that set off our panic and reactivity—and what to do when they get irritated. We'll also explore techniques for listening to other people and for telling people how we want to be listened to, as well as how to apologize and forgive. These conflict skills can build strength in our relationships, and I will offer ideas about how to notice when that building is happening—and how to develop and maintain these strengths.

We All Have Sore Spots

Bennie and Tobias have been in a community group for five years and are planning a conference together, which requires weekly meetings and a number of shared tasks. They are friends and have shared values, but they frequently set each other off in meetings. Bennie gets easily agitated when she thinks a plan the group is discussing won't work, and she can become explosive and demanding. When people act like that around Tobias, he feels a strong reaction of "don't tell me what to do!" rooted in his experience of being raised by an overly controlling caregiver. Tobias often goes silent when Bennie explodes, and then Bennie feels judged and worried that Tobias doesn't like her—or, worse, that no one likes her.

The concept of having sore spots can help us notice and name what sets off our insecurity or panic.[1] For some of us, it might be a tone we hear in another's voice; for others, it is a phrase. For instance, I hate being told to "calm down." That simple phrase sets off a strong shame reaction in me. My friend Katrina, however, experiences road rage and *likes* that her girlfriend can help her by telling her to "calm down." Our differing reactions to this phrase illustrate how specific these cues are for each of us. We are all wildly different from each other and cannot expect others to know what sets us off unless we explicitly tell them. Even then, we can't expect others to remember our sore spots perfectly.

There are endless examples of sore spots. Some people can't stand to be corrected about the way they speak. Some people feel terrified if anyone says they are disappointed by something they did. Some people freeze up whenever anyone's voice is raised. Some are hypersensitive to any comment that implies they aren't smart or competent. Some people are extra sensitive about money matters, or their birthday, or being left out, or being perceived as lazy. Are there things you know are sore spots for you, things that throw you into a strong reaction?

When someone rubs your sore spot, often there is a physical sensation: your stomach churns, your back tenses; your breathing changes or the blood rushes to your face. Some people might get hot and sweaty; others will experience numbness, or lightheadedness. We might feel an impulse to fight, flee, or hide—or to try to appease the other person at any cost. Identifying patterns in your responses can help reduce the autopilot reaction—you can notice what is happening consciously rather than being swept away by it. It can also help you explain to others what is happening, and ask for their compassion and support.[2]

If I notice that when a partner's other lover comes up in conversation I sometimes feel sweaty and want to leave, I can catch myself before I obey those insecurity reactions. I can explain what's happening, and ask for a hug or a moment alone. Knowing what is happening and being transparent about it, rather than expressing it through withdrawal or an unkind comment, can prevent damage to the connection.

Telling those close to us about our sore spots can help them know how to care for us. Knowing our own sore spots and telling loved ones also helps us take responsibility for our own feelings and experiences. When we share our sore spots with loved ones, it does not mean that they will perfectly avoid them, or that others are "bad" if they accidentally rub the sore spot again. It is simply information that they can try to remember and use to inform their interactions with us. Similarly, knowing our own sore spots helps us act with care, rather than lashing out or casting blame when we feel a strong reaction bubbling up. The point is not to come up with a list of taboos that loved ones must never violate or areas they can never give feedback about. Rather, it is a chance to help others understand, build compassion for, and practice care with us. Our reactions are, ultimately, our own responsibility. The goal of noticing and sharing sore spots is to learn about our reactions, so we can navigate them, and ask very specifically for support, knowing that it is all right if the person cannot give it or cannot always give it perfectly.

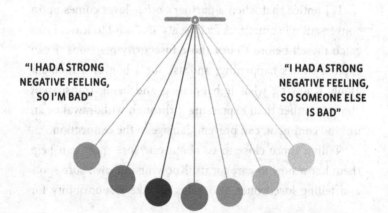

"I HAD A STRONG NEGATIVE FEELING, SO I'M BAD"

"I HAD A STRONG NEGATIVE FEELING, SO SOMEONE ELSE IS BAD"

When strong feelings come up, many of us jump to one of the two ends of the spectrum illustrated above. We may have thoughts like these (on the left):

* I'm too sensitive.

* I need to get my shit together and act normal.

* I'm damaged and broken.

These thoughts blame and shame ourselves for having sore spots.

Or we may have thoughts like (on the right):

* You said something no one should ever say.

* You know that hurts me. You are trying to hurt me.

These thoughts blame others for our sore spots, insisting that they tiptoe around them, or they assume that everyone finds the same things provoking.

LEARNING ABOUT SORE spots can reduce reactivity. If we know it and name it as such, then when someone rubs against it, we both know the reaction is not about them, so both of us are less likely to escalate with blame and defensiveness. If a loved one tells you they have a sore spot, then if you accidentally set it off, you can focus on being compassionate during their reaction instead of taking it personally. Learning about our sore spots can also increase flexibility, especially if we don't make inflexible demands on other people's behaviors.

The more we notice sore spots, the less intense they might become, so that something you were once rigid about—never being corrected in a certain way, say—might become less of a big deal.

Learning about our sore spots is one way to see through the surface content of conflict and to begin to understand the insecurity that drives those moments of panic. When Mustafa and Jozi fight about his punctuality on game nights, her fears of abandonment are stirred—why doesn't he care enough to come home on time?—and she becomes rigid about her bedtime as a way to rationalize her panic. Her criticism of him is really a plea for contact.

Mustafa, on the other hand, fears engulfment, feels unappreciated for how he has accommodated her requests, feels resentment for where he has overextended to try to meet her needs. He rationalizes it as wanting her to support his time with his brothers, but the bigger underlying fear is that she doesn't support his autonomy and love him for who he is, rather than as someone to control. Rather than asserting his needs about coming home later, he keeps promising an early return and then failing to do it. They are caught in a cycle of rubbing each other's sore spots and escalating the reactivity between them.

Perhaps learning that you don't want to spend New Year's Eve with him made your lover feel like he's not important to you. Perhaps when you disagreed with your friend in the meeting, she suddenly felt like you didn't have her back and that she was alone in the group. At these moments we might become hypercritical around the content of the argument, or become avoidant and disappear. The more we can learn about our and others' sore spots and reaction patterns, the more we can navigate these moments of activation without piling on more hurt and loss. If we know what makes us feel loved and seen and learn how to ask for what we want, we can build—or rebuild—satisfying relationships where we feel security and love. We live in difficult and terrifying times. We need to be able to build relationships where we feel supported, so we can do what is needed to survive and resist together.

* Could you imagine telling someone about your sore spots? How would you want them to respond?
* How can you tell the difference between universally hurtful things and sore spots specific to you?
* Are you aware of any of your loved ones' sore spots? Are there ways you could show more compassion and care for them when you are in conflict?

The Four Horsemen of the Apocalypse

Over twenty years ago, psychotherapist John Gottman famously identified four behaviors that are strong predictors of breakup. Regardless of whether we are thinking about a romantic or other kind of relationship, and regardless of whether we are worried about breakup, these behaviors undermine trust[3] and are worth looking out for:

* Personal Criticism, which includes blame and attacking someone's character or personality.
* Defensiveness, which includes denying their experience or justifying our actions.
* Contempt, which is an attitude of demeaning, disrespecting, mocking, or undermining someone else.
* Stonewalling, which includes avoiding people and/or giving the silent treatment.

Are these happening in any of your relationships? Did you see these in your childhood caregivers? What does it feel like to be on either side of these? These can be a reminder about how we want to treat each other, that even in conflict we don't want to engage in behaviors that undermine trust and connection, and when we do behave this way, we take seriously the need for apology and repair.

When Your Sore Spot Gets Rubbed

Cherie and Tre opened their relationship six months ago and are enjoying sex with new people and the aliveness that this has brought to their connection. Cherie very much wants an open relationship but also struggles with jealousy. Yesterday, she was looking at pictures someone posted of a party, and she saw one of Tre kissing someone else. Tre was not violating any of their agreements, but Cherie still felt shocked, numb, angry, and afraid.

Cherie notices her patterns, and could identify her fear of abandonment being activated. These feelings don't change their shared commitment to nonmonogamy, and they've agreed to connect with care when hard feelings come up. Cherie told Tre how she was feeling and asked him to hold her. Cherie was proud of not lashing out or criticizing Tre, and Tre felt good about being compassionate and present rather than defensive. After a few minutes of holding each other, Cherie's reaction started to calm, and they relaxed into each other.

If you have ever suddenly encountered giant feelings—anger, jealousy, loneliness, abandonment, or the urge to get out and never come back—you have probably had a sore spot get rubbed. If you can take a minute to think, "I am having a big emotional reaction," rather than only being *inside* that reaction (experiencing thoughts like, "Nobody wants me,"

"They are all out to get me," "This is his fault," or "This place is bullshit, I'm leaving") you have already taken a step toward support for your wounded self.

Often, we struggle to see that we are having an emotional reaction. It can be hard to remember that, although a moment *feels* like life-or-death, it is actually a bunch of stirred-up feelings that deserve our love and attention, and won't always feel this bad. We might only learn to notice our reactivity because someone else points out the pattern and its impacts. That can spur us to learn to notice the feelings rather than being taken over by them and having them direct our behavior. This is one of the ways that relationships help us to emotionally mature and heal—people give us feedback.

We want to shift from blaming others for our experiences—using indicting or criticizing language—toward describing what is happening internally. When we share our feelings with others, it is important to use *feeling words*. Feeling words include: lonely, helpless, frustrated, uncomfortable, guarded, scared, hurt, hopeless, helpless, panicked, inadequate, alone, confused, lost, embarrassed, ashamed, blank, afraid, shocked, sad, forlorn, numb, humiliated, overwhelmed, small, vulnerable, worried.

Remember that big feelings do not come strictly from what others are doing, but from our own prior wounds being stimulated by our interactions with others. Ideally, we move away from "You made me feel this way because you are bad" and toward "I am having these feelings and I would like to talk about them and be heard by you."

A useful method for this kind of sharing is called Nonviolent Communication, which you can read more about on p. 241.[4] In this method, the sharer is encouraged to describe what she observed, factually, and how she felt, subjectively, but to avoid characterizing the *other* person.

It can be terrifying to share a feeling. "I can't possibly share this" is a sore spot reaction like the others discussed above. If you are scared, talking to a friend or therapist in a confidential space or visiting an in-person or online support group (such as a grief support group, or a group for survivors of violence) can be a useful starting place. We may fear that others will minimize, dismiss, or judge our feelings. If we have repressed strong feelings for a long time, we may worry that once we open the door, these emotions will flood in and overpower us. These are normal fears, and it can help to look at our situation, evaluate the cost of not letting ourselves feel things fully, and try to notice what support we have as we dip our toes into feeling.

* Can you think of a time when you blamed someone for a strong reaction after they accidentally rubbed one of your sore spots? What happened? What would you do differently if you were in that situation again?

* Do you worry that if you start noticing sore spots, you
  won't be able to function? What helps soothe that fear?
* Why is it worth letting yourself feel more, and sharing
  your feelings with people in your life?

Listening

*Mustafa talked with his best friend, Nina, about the
tensions with Jozi, and Nina encouraged him to express
his feelings to Jozi directly at a time when they are not
fighting—so they both might be more open and relaxed.
Last weekend, after a walk in the park, Mustafa told Jozi
that he feels like he needs more time alone. It didn't go
well. At first Jozi kept looking at her phone, distracted.
Then, once she realized what Mustafa was saying, she
crossed her arms and looked angry. He clammed up,
then it turned into a fight. Jozi tried to get Mustafa to
say what he really wanted, and he told her he wanted
to just leave the conversation alone. They both felt
awful after.*

In my experience, most people think they are good listeners, but few of us are. When we choose to tell someone something vulnerable, it is important to think about whether they
will be a good listener. We can also actively work to improve
our own listening skills. Some of the keys to good listening are:

* **Not giving advice:** Perhaps the most common listening mistake is advice-giving. Most people want support, not advice. Advice can feel paternalistic or impatient, as if you are trying to "solve" a person's feelings for them. It's better to focus on witnessing and empathizing and give advice only if asked.

* **Focusing on the other person:** Many of us have a tendency to shift the attention back to our stories, rather than truly listening. If it feels important to share our story, we can always do it at another time, after first giving our full attention to what this person is sharing—and not planning what *we* are going to say next.

* **Mirroring:** Many people use body language to demonstrate attention (a forward body posture; eye contact if appropriate; expressions of affirmation and encouragement), but we can also show people we are listening by *reflecting back* what we have heard. Especially during conflict, this lets the other person experience being heard. We can repeat back what they said into our own words and ask, "Did I get that right?"

* **Touch:** Mindful physical contact can show support and connection. Asking a person if they want to be touched, and exactly what kinds of touch would feel right, can be supportive and loving. Remember that this varies, and that social conditions, abuse histories, gender norms, and stigmas (for example, against people with disabilities and old people), often shape access to touch and desire for touch.

Listening can be difficult. When someone is sharing strong feelings. especially if they were stimulated by an inter-action with us, our emotions get stirred, too. Hearing a friend or loved one express pain may make us want to make their feelings stop. Hearing that they are in pain because of some-thing we said or did can lead us to feel defensive. Ideally, we can notice these impulses but still choose to keep the focus on listening—demonstrating for the other person our care and witnessing.

When someone characterizes an event or experience in a way we disagree with or remember differently, we can still choose to listen and reflect. Offering a "correction" in the moment will probably continue the conflict spiral. A com-mon example of this is when people fight about the quantity of something: how often you did the dishes, how often we had sex, etc. Instead, we need to compassionately bear witness, listening for their needs for security and support. If we can lovingly hear another's experience and reflect it back to them, *it does not mean we are agreeing that we experienced it the same way.* It just means that we care about what it was like for them.

Being heard satisfies deep needs in us. This can build trust and safety and generate more flexibility and resilience. It can help us heal from the very childhood experiences that created the sore spots in the first place. When we practice this kind of care in friendships and other relationships, it helps us create the systems of support we need so desperately.

* Do you have relationships in which you are scared to share your feelings because the other person has judged, dismissed, or strongly reacted to such sharing before?
* Are there some relationships where this fear might *not* be justified, but is a holdover from other experiences?
* What about when people have been good listeners? Are there ways you like to be listened to that you could share with loved ones? Are there things that you've noticed good listeners do that you want to try when you are listening?

On Nonviolent Communication

Nonviolent Communication (NVC) is the name of a tool for communicating that can build skills for giving and receiving feedback. (N.B.: Its name is a sticking point for me, as someone who is critical of how the liberal rhetoric of "nonviolence" justifies the criminalization of armed movements for self-defense and self-determination by colonized and oppressed people.[5])

NVC encourages us to share our observations and feelings, rather than accusations or generalizations about the other person. For example, if my date did not text me back in time to finalize our plans, I might share, "You did not text me back, and I felt worried that you don't want to hang out." I do not say anything about *what the person is like*, for example, "You're inconsiderate, and you don't care about me as much as I care about you."

Generalizations make the other person unlikely to listen, reduce them to one dehumanizing adjective, and can lead to fights in which people are keeping score. The NVC model focuses on what you observed, and how you feel. You don't know what the experience was like for the other person or what their reasons may have been.

NVC also recommends asking people when might be a good time to share feedback, and having the person receiving feedback agree to just listen. Asking for consent before sharing feedback establishes that you care about their experience—perhaps they would prefer to talk when they are better rested, for instance. Establishing that the feedback receiver will just listen for now can help prevent immediate defensiveness that escalates conflict. After the feedback has been heard and after the listener has mirrored back what they heard, they can ask whether the sharer wants to hear their experience at that time or another time. These two *different* conversations need not happen in one session.

While I have not adopted the formal NVC model in my daily life (there is more to this than I am including here), learning about NVC has helped me avoid making generalizations about others when giving feedback or sharing my hard feelings. I also try not to say "always" or "never" when characterizing what I observe, since it's rarely accurate and tends to escalate conflict. Like any other tool, people can misuse or even weaponize NVC. Good faith, along with a genuine desire to hear and care for the other person or people and a commitment to take responsibility for our own emotional activation, is the baseline for any conflict resolution and repair.

Apologizing

Lorenzo and Billy have been hooking up for a couple months, usually at night after the bars close. Last weekend, Billy fell asleep at Lorenzo's and ended up staying over. In the morning, Lorenzo was stressed because his boyfriend was coming over, and, despite their open relationship, he didn't want his boyfriend to run into Billy unexpectedly.

He was a bit curt, trying to get Billy out the door, and didn't tell Billy why he was rushing him out. Billy felt embarrassed and pissed at Lorenzo's behavior. Later in the day he texted: "Hey, that was kind of rude this morning." Lorenzo didn't write back. Now Billy feels weird going to social spaces where he might run into Lorenzo.

We all make mistakes in relationships. We run late, forget birthdays, fail to do our part of some work we agreed to do, make thoughtless comments. We get activated in our fears, think someone else is the enemy, and criticize or withdraw in hurtful ways. Our racist, capitalist, colonial society relies on simplistic binaries. We internalize the good person/bad person binary and live in fear of being a bad person. We imagine that if others think we are bad, we might be cast out. We live in a prison society where being cast out is a valid concern, and where widespread belief in fictions about "good people" and "bad people" normalize practices like putting humans in cages.

One result of this conditioning is that we have a hard time recognizing when we have made mistakes, admitting them, and then apologizing authentically. We fearfully defend ourselves, and from that place, we have a hard time seeing ourselves as capable of hurting others. If we practice authentic apology in the day-to-day, we can hone our skills for the bigger hurts that inevitably come up in important relationships. As you read about apologies below, try to be curious about your current relationship to apologizing without judging yourself, even if you find areas for improvement.

Ineffective apologies can include:

* Very short apologies. "Yeah, sorry. But moving on . . ."
* Apologies that minimize what happened. "Well, maybe I did that but . . ."
* Apologies that sound forced. "I guess I am supposed to say I am sorry . . ."
* Instrumental apologies. "Nothing is going to work until I say this so . . ."

An effective apology should include the following:

* This is what I did.
* I care about how it impacted you. Here is what I heard you say about how the impact felt.
* Your feelings are legitimate.
* I regret this action.
* This is how I will avoid doing it again.[6]

There is a risk both in being too defensive or too willing to take responsibility. Defensiveness is easy to spot in the crappy apologies above. However, being too willing to take responsibility can also be a way to evade accountability. When we get an overdone apology from someone who apologizes for everything, it can feel as unsatisfying as no apology. When a friend misses our birthday and then says "I'm the worst person ever; you should never forgive me," it can seem like a demand for us to reassure them with something like: "That's okay; it's no problem." A satisfying apology that builds trust is right-sized for the harm. In a culture where often harm is either minimized or punishment and exile are invoked, we have a lot to learn about proportionate responses to mistakes.

Do you take too little or too much responsibility? Do you take too little with your lover and too much with your family? Investigating how and when we do and don't apologize can reveal patterns of over- and under-accountability. Finding balance in apologizing means respecting both our own dignity and integrity *and* the dignity and integrity of the person we are apologizing to.

* Have you had any satisfying experiences of apologizing or being apologized to? What made them satisfying?
* What could you improve about how you apologize?

Forgiveness

Six months after Lorenzo and Billy had that unplanned sleepover, the police shot a young person in their town and Billy joined the organizing in response. Lorenzo was already active in the anti-racist coalition, and when he saw Billy at one of their meetings, he realized it might be awkward. Not wanting Billy to feel like he couldn't be part of the work because of what had happened between them, Lorenzo asked Billy to go for coffee and talk. He apologized for ghosting and said that he realized he did not handle their morning together well. He told Billy he wanted him to feel comfortable in the organizing meetings. Billy would have simply avoided their history, but felt more trust because of how Lorenzo apologized.

There is almost no template for repair in our society. Our punishment-focused culture gives us few skills for acknowledging mistakes, apologizing, or forgiving. Many of us have had experiences of pretending something wasn't harmful or didn't happen at all. Or we have felt pressured to tell someone we forgive them, even though their apology felt inadequate.

Real repair processes include: telling someone that they hurt you; hearing them understand the impact of their actions and how they plan to avoid repeating them; and hearing them truly apologize. On the other side, it looks like: hearing someone share that you hurt them; genuinely reflecting on it; acknowledging the impact you had on them; and apologizing for your actions, including sharing how you plan to avoid doing this again. Forgiving and being forgiven, even about small things, can change us. It can give us a new faith that we can actually recover from the ubiquitous violations we experience in this brutal culture. It can help us imagine how a world might function where people have safety and well-being without punishment systems.

When my boyfriend got sober seven years into our relationship, I suddenly felt a great deal of resentment about all the times his drinking had impacted me. While it was going on, I held much of my resentment at bay, often lost in "just get by" mechanisms I adopted from my childhood experience living with an alcoholic parent. But when he got sober, all my resentment came rushing in. I needed help to forgive him. A couples therapist recommended we do a process in our sessions with her in which I shared with him stories from his drinking that were still painful and he repeated them back to me. Hearing the words directly from his mouth, I finally felt that he heard my experiences and was genuinely apologizing. I was surprised by how effective the method was.

After years of classic alcoholic amnesia—during which he didn't seem to remember all the times he'd made similar mistakes—it was a relief to have him acknowledge the ways his behavior hurt me. Feeling heard and seeing his pain at taking in what he had done, I felt increased compassion for him. We did two or three sessions like this, and after those sessions we replayed the exercise whenever we needed to, on matters big or small, without the therapist. Months and years after he became sober, if something brought up a painful story we had never discussed, I would check to see if it was an okay time to share what was on my mind, and if it was, I would tell him the story and he would mirror it back.

Practicing made the conversations strangely light—he didn't get defensive, I didn't feel like I needed to exaggerate anything about the story or my pain to feel heard. Eventually, the stories surfaced less and less in my mind, and when they did, they didn't feel particularly charged. I could really let go of what had happened during those years.

I have come to realize that this was the first genuine experience of forgiveness of my life. Most of us don't ever get to do this with any of our big conflicts—with our families, at jobs, or with breakups. I experienced true forgiveness—no longer haunted by resentments or afraid of him repeating the behavior. Most important, I knew that if he did relapse, I could trust myself to make decisions for my own well-being, to hold my boundaries, which were new skills that came from this process.

Five years into practicing this kind of forgiveness, my boyfriend lied to me about maintaining our safer sex agreements (our relationship was nonmonogamous). I could see why he did it—how it was part of his own emotional activation. The lie related directly both to his childhood experiences with keeping secrets in order to feel autonomy from an over-intervening parent, and to his adult journey, in which expressing his sexuality was instrumental to healing. I knew it was not intended to hurt me, and that he was not even entirely aware he was lying. It had no material impact on my life or health, and I had no objections to changing our agreement, but of course, I was angry and hurt because he lied. I felt that my agency was being taken away and that he was trying to control my reality, nonconsensually casting me in a parental role in his internal drama. I let him know that being lied to is a deal-breaker for me. He did the work to figure out why he had lied, and apologized meaningfully.

Throughout the whole process, I was much less emotionally activated than I would have been in the past. I could imagine a past version of myself labeling him "a liar" in my mind. But the truth was now clear to me: he is honest in 99 percent of our life together, and in one area, his coping responses from childhood came up, causing him to act outside his values. I could hold the whole reality of him with love while also drawing a clear line about what I needed. I felt secure in my own ability to hold my boundaries and not be a doormat, and I felt able to know when he had heard me and we could move on. For me, our forgiveness work had built this possibility. I could keep myself safe, even though he is imperfect and growing and may continue to make mistakes that hurt me.

The truth is that we can never guarantee that someone will be trustworthy. We all try our best to act on our principles and do what we have promised, but we fall down. When we forgive someone, we do not know for certain what their future behavior will be. When they show an understanding of their impact (even if they do not agree with us on every element of what happened), we move forward knowing that we will give feedback again if we have to. Our trust lies not just in the other person, but in our own ability to make ourselves safe and whole.

If you are in a situation where you want to work on forgiveness but the other person is unwilling or unavailable (estranged, deceased, incapable of hearing about their impact), you can still do forgiveness work. You can cultivate all the elements of the forgiveness process within yourself. These include:

* Acknowledging that hurt or harm happened. Having compassion for yourself about the hurt.
* Acknowledging any long-term impact on you.
* Thinking about what actions you might take to protect yourself from this happening again, if any are possible. How can you generate more safety for yourself in similar situations, knowing what you know now?
* Connecting to any compassion you have for the person who hurt you. Is there anything you know about why they might have done this that you can understand compassionately?

The key to this kind of forgiveness, or any forgiveness, is that it cannot be forced or rushed. It is okay if the forgiveness is partial. Perhaps you can let go of one part of it. Perhaps you can feel compassion for one aspect of the person. Most of us, as we work to build better relationships by cultivating emotional awareness and acknowledging childhood shaping, will need to do this work with regard to our childhood caregivers, whether or not they are able to engage with us about it.

* Have you had any authentic experiences of being forgiven or forgiving someone else? What worked in those instances?
* Are there people you would like to forgive?
* Are there any ways you would like to forgive yourself?

Maintaining Connection

Mei and Honey are best friends who used to date. Honey is more social and busy, and Mei sometimes worries that Honey doesn't care about their friendship as much as she does. Honey does care deeply about Mei, and sometimes feels unappreciated, wondering why Mei can't trust how much their relationship means to them.

They share consistent rituals: hosting a big party for Lunar New Year, and camping, just the two of them, every August. And they text each other a "goodnight meme" almost every night. These little things help them both feel connected, and have eased fear and conflict between them over the years.

Most relationship self-help advice is focused on feeling secure and supported in romantic partnerships, but it is radical and transformative to also actively cultivate these feelings in other relationships. Having security anywhere in our lives can help us feel more secure across all of our connections.

To maintain our connections in both romance and friendship, we can cultivate awareness of our sore spots and find ways out of reactivity, and learn to find support for strong feelings when they come up. We can also celebrate moments of connection. Did you feel loved when your friend picked you up from the doctor? When your roommate left you a packed lunch? When your collaborator remembered to ask about your grandmother's surgery?

The moments when we feel cared for are worth sharing with the person who gave us the love and support. We can also mark our separations and reunions—many of us have sore spots around those—with rituals, as a way of acknowledging the importance of the relationship to both people.

HERE ARE SOME specific suggestions[7] that might spark your own ideas for maintaining connection and building a feeling of security. These could be done with family, friends, roommates, lovers, or collaborators, as appropriate to your situation:

* Regular special meals (like a certain day of the week)
* A special weekly or monthly time to hang out
* Seasonal garden planting or other outdoor time
* Attending community events together that mark time or seasons or have contemplative space

* Setting aside time to share about how you are doing if this tends to get lost—after dinner on Mondays, or right before bed, or a special phone call time, whatever makes sense
* Holding, hugging, or kissing upon waking, going to sleep, leaving, returning, or reuniting
* Taking a class or some other learning activity together, reading a book together
* Leaving each other notes, especially when someone is going away or after time of distance or disagreement
* Paying attention to special anniversaries, birthdays, and other significant dates by doing something personal and meaningful to mark them
* Acknowledging the other person's struggles and affirming their efforts: "that was hard for you and you really followed through"; "I saw you struggling there and you really showed up"
* Recognizing the relationship in ways that would be feel good to you (friendiversary parties, matching tattoos, a special food or drink, etc.)

In general, when we openly appreciate each other, we can cultivate feelings that the relationships are reliable, are sites of support, and are important to all involved. For people who feel avoidant or withdrawing, some of these things may seem unappealing or even smothering. But we can explore whether there is a way to enjoy and connect with these activities, choosing activities that work for both parties. What would make it feel like a choice rather than an obligation?

For example, one of my best friends is bad at gift-giving on a schedule. We have agreed that there is no pressure to give birthday or holiday gifts at any time. This allows us to enjoy our connection around special dates more, because there is no pressure or sense of obligation hanging over us and creating disconnection. Similarly, I have friends who feel avoidant around correspondence. Talking about it, agreeing that there is no pressure to respond, or that I will indicate if something is time sensitive, allows them to relax, rather than getting activated and disappearing.

It is easier to give and receive love when there is a shared sense of flexibility, and when we can name avoidant tendencies without judgment. I think it is particularly important for people who feel avoidant to not do things they don't want to do. If we cannot say no to each other, it becomes hard to find an authentic yes. Avoidant reactions are more likely to spike when we try to force things, and more likely to melt away when there is less pressure.

* Do any of the suggested activities for maintaining connection remind you of things you already do with loved ones?
* Do they give you any ideas of things that might be useful to try?

Acknowledging When It Works

Last New Year's Eve, Mei and Honey had a misunderstanding. Mei thought they were going to spend the holiday together, start to finish, and Honey thought they were both going to the same party but might go their separate ways at the end of the night. Honey was excited to meet their crush at the party, and hoped to take the crush home.

The day before the party, during a conversation about their plans, Honey and Mei realized they had different assumptions about the night. Mei shared that she was disappointed, and Honey shared that they felt worried that Mei would be mad. They were both able to describe their feelings and hear each other, and see how the misunderstanding was an honest mistake. By the end of the conversation, they felt reconnected, and made plans to meet before the party to get dressed together.

If you have a successful moment of reconnecting after conflict, it can be helpful to write down what went well. What helped us move toward connection and support rather than getting stuck in fears and autopilot responses? Your notes might include a few words on each of these questions:[8]

* How did the relationship feel when it was stalled in insecurity or negative spirals? (e.g., dead-ended, exhausting, a minefield)

* How do each of you usually move in the dynamic when it's stuck? (e.g., you criticize, I retreat)
* How did the two of you do something different? (e.g., You shared your fears instead of criticizing, I reached out and offered you reassurance instead of avoiding you.)
* What was one moment when you saw each other differently, felt new emotions and/or were able to reach for each other? (e.g., I hugged you instead of walking out of the room, I called you instead of avoiding you, I sat beside you in connected silence instead of criticizing.)
* How does it feel now that we came through it? (e.g., peaceful, playful, connected)[9]

This exercise is designed for people in the relationship to do together, but I think we can also use this style of reflection by ourselves, in order to notice outcomes when we try new things. You could also do this as a mapping exercise, drawing a map of where your reactions usually take you and what you did or would like to do differently in the future. Reflecting on a new experience increases the likelihood that we will remember it and that it will be an option when autopilot tries to pull us back into our old approach. When we've been practicing certain emotional reactions and behaviors for years, it takes conscious practice to make a change.

For years I had a pattern where whenever I was in a meeting and the group identified a task that needed to be done, I would feel a strong impulse to volunteer for the task. It stemmed from my unconscious desire to be seen as useful, and to secure my place in the group by being of service. It also often included a tinge of anxiety that the work either wouldn't get done, or wouldn't get done in what I thought was the "right" way. This pattern sometimes resulted in overwork, exhaustion, and neglect of other parts of my life. I made a map for myself of other things I can do to prepare when that impulse comes on.

Now I assess my current capacity before I go into a meeting, and decide ahead of time what I can reasonably take on. I sometimes enlist a friend who will be there to keep me accountable, if I worry I won't be able to keep to my plan. Sometimes I use an internal guideline. For example, if a task comes up, I won't volunteer to take it on until at least three other people have spoken. Sometimes, for motivation, I'll make a list of things I'd do if I had more free time in order to remember what new commitments might be taking me away from.

You could also make a map for predictably sticky moments in your relationships. Let's say you often experience jealousy when you first see your lover after they return from a date with someone else. You don't mean to, and you know it's not wise, but you ask questions about their date, and sometimes you say critical or judgmental things in response to what you learn. This hurts your lover and causes conflict, and you feel bad about it after. You have agreed to consensual nonmonogamy and you want your lover to be able to feel good about their dates, not punished when you get back together; you also know your jealousy stems from a fear of abandonment.

Instead of letting that jealous reaction take over, try something new. Maybe when you first see each other, you could ask for some nonverbal time to feel physically close, hugging or making out, to experience connection. Maybe you could take a walk or play a game, while agreeing not to start talking about their recent dates until you are feeling reconnected. Identifying how an interaction usually goes, and thinking through alternate approaches outside the heat of the moment, takes care of our future selves.

Perhaps you can imagine a repeating situation that kicks up autopilot reactions you would like to change: a visit from your relatives, running into your partner's ex, disagreeing with a date about money? For any situation where you might be in need of a new plan, you can work ahead of time on mapping other options you might have, and you can make notes or tell a friend about the results after you try something different. These efforts can help us have more choices to practice new things. Check out the Mad Mapping Jealousy exercise on p. 307 for further inspiration on how to do this.

/// ? ///

* Can you think of times when you have felt supported
  while experiencing insecurity?
* Are there any takeaways about what works that you
  want to remember or share with loved ones?
* Can you think of a repeating situation that stirs autopilot
  reactions that you could map to avoid some of those
  patterned behaviors?

///

Attachment to Others and Feeling Ourselves

*Last year, Jacky and their boyfriend moved across the
country to take care of Jacky's elderly aunt. Their relationship was already on the rocks, and the move pushed
it over the edge and their boyfriend left. Jacky ended
up living in a town where they don't know people, relatively isolated because they need to be with their aunt
most of the time. There were hard things about this,
but also some gifts. They weren't around peers much,
and they felt strangely free. They started experiment-
ing with how they dressed and groomed, and trying to
play silly pop songs using their aunt's piano. For the first
time in their life, they weren't rushing around being
social and working a lot; they weren't trying to look
sexy and desirable for anyone besides themself. When
they met some people after a while at a karaoke night,*

*they realized they felt a lot more relaxed and confident
than they had before this period of greater solitude and
self-experimentation.*

This work isn't just about relating with others; it is also
about becoming more aware and accepting of ourselves.

Living in cultures of domination and violence, many of us
become disconnected from ourselves, while trying to fit into
rigid cultural norms. Under constant threat of punishment,
many of us focus on extrinsic approval for a sense of safety.
This can impact our ability to know what we really want, or
even what we feel, because we have repressed so much of ourselves to get by in families, at school, and in jobs. Some of
us end up doing things out of obligation; some of us pursue
things that don't satisfy when we get them. Some have a hard
time prioritizing our own desires over doing what others
want. Automatic emotional settings and habits make it hard
to establish good boundaries with people, jobs, and projects,
and because of this overdeveloped external focus and underdeveloped sense of ourselves, a great deal of our healing must
emphasize building deeper *internal* connections.

This, of course, requires work. Contemplative practices
like reading books about emotional experiences and growth,
working with therapists, and meditating can help. Doing
body-based work, like somatic therapy, singing, dance, yoga,
sports, can also be part of this. Practices that are about being
alone rather than about performing for others—such as solo

retreats, doing hobbies we are not striving to be "good" at, journaling, art making, or spiritual practices—can cultivate a sense of self. For many of us, basic boundary-setting practices—having a bedtime and eating regularly, or creating a clear structure for saying yes or no to new obligations—can help us remember that our experiences matter, rather than trying to get security from outside ourselves.

It is important to affirm the centrality of building relationships with ourselves when learning about building security with others, just as it is important that we expand the focus of this work beyond romantic relationships to include other important relationships. Building a greater sense of security so that we can reduce our reactivity and deepen our connections to others and ourselves does not require being in a romantic partnership or any other particular kind of relationship. The work is about emotional awareness in ourselves, interest in what underlies strong feelings, and building compassion as we explore patterns and autopilot settings from early wounds. Stopping persistent cycles of conflict in intimate relationships is a significant benefit of these efforts, but ideally this work enhances connections and a sense of security and choice in all areas of our lives. In Chapter Six, we'll look at some of the nuts and bolts of negotiating with people in our lives about how we want to connect, given what we know about how rocky the terrain can be. We'll move deeper into imagining what our lives can look like if we have robust support systems and shared, passionate commitments to connection and liberation.

Chapter Five Recap

* We all have sore spots—things that bring up big reactions in us. They are unique to every person, so we can't expect others to predict them, nor can we blame others when they accidentally rub up against them.

* Telling other people about our sore spots can help them have compassion for us when we are having strong feelings, and may help them avoid rubbing these places. But we cannot expect others to always remember our sore spots. Our reactions are our responsibility.

* Learning how to listen to others—and telling each other how we want to be listened to—can generate connection and make conflict less heated. Good listening means showing with words or body language that we are listening, staying focused on the speaker, and not rushing to give advice.

* A good apology shows that you understand what the other person is saying about their experience, acknowledges the impact of your actions, and explains how you plan to avoid repeating the mistake.

* Experiences of genuine forgiveness are rare and profoundly healing. It doesn't work to rush forgiveness. We can do forgiveness work even if the other person isn't available to engage with us or apologize.

* This healing work is about connecting to others, but it requires that we increase our connections to ourselves, learning who we are and what we want, and believing that that matters.

Revolutionary Promiscuity— Getting Free Together

///

> The role of the artist is exactly the same as the role of the lover. If I love you, I have to make you conscious of things you don't see.
>
> —JAMES BALDWIN

> An army of lovers cannot fail.
>
> —ACT UP

Makeda has been reading more books about anti-capitalism, Black freedom, and feminism lately. She works in business school admissions, and is thinking about quitting her job because she doesn't believe in what they teach. She's done with mistreatment from her non-Black coworkers.

When she shares her plans with her mom and her boyfriend, they don't get it. Her mom doesn't want her to quit a stable job or make her life harder by becoming politically active. Her boyfriend dislikes that Makeda is changing so much, and can't understand why she isn't happy with the good job and the good life they've built together. Makeda knows they love her, but wishes she had someone to talk with who has read the same books and would listen to her ideas.

I'VE OFTEN WISHED we could treat our friends more like lovers and our lovers more like friends. In defiance of the romance myth, I want us to pour our attention and care and generosity into our friendships, rather than ditching them carelessly when romance calls. At the same time, I wish we could hold our sex and dating relationships more lightly, caring about them and being good to each other, but disentangling from the romance myth idea that this is where we are supposed to get *all* our love and support. So much of the harm that unfolds within sexual and romantic relationships comes from this tight grip, the ways our sense of worth—and our fears of engulfment and abandonment—get exceptionally stirred up by lovers.

When I imagine real freedom and liberation in our relationships, we are holding each other with tenderness and realistic expectations. True intimacy means we work to see each other not just through the projections of perfection and wish fulfillment (during the early phases) and then disappointment and blame (as conflict arrives), but instead as the complex, flawed, exquisitely gorgeous beings that we are. This means accepting, compassionately, that we will perceive reality differently—especially around our sore spots. It means accepting that we will love each other imperfectly, that we all must give and receive feedback, and that none of us is entirely aware of our motivations. We must accept, with compassion, that none of us is living perfectly in line with our values or intentions, and we must support our efforts toward alignment.

Relationships will hit bumps, transform, and even end— all valuable parts of being alive. We must shed the capitalist imperial fantasies of "forever" that the romance myth feeds us through its ties to the state marriage system. We can't get safe, or free, by locking things down and punishing people when they rub us the wrong way. Despite what the romance myth tells us, no one else can make us permanently happy. Rather, cultivating feelings of emotional satisfaction, connection, belonging, and creativity is an ongoing process we are in with ourselves, our friends, lovers, collaborators, family members, and even our enemies. I want to see us in relationships where we can feel high regard for others and desire others' growth and well-being in the same way that we desire our own. We must understand that our life paths are tied together, but they are not knowable or predictable.

To survive in any conditions, but especially during ecological crises, war, sharply rising wealth inequality, murderously profit-driven healthcare and housing systems, we need robust interpersonal support networks. We need as many people as possible to have our backs—not just lovers. I want all of us to have abundant support, as many people as we want to share food, make art, have sex, play, and read with, people who will care for us when we are sick or heartbroken.

Isolation makes every bad thing that can happen to us more dangerous. Connection makes survival and healing possible.

Rather than exclusivity, where we get our key needs met through just one or a few relationships, we need promiscuous support systems, so that when things change in any one of our relationships or we can't get what we need from any particular person or group, we can still find the connections we need. Would it be possible to have the best aspects of friendship—freedom, mutual regard, acceptance of differences, honesty, non-possessive loyalty—combined with the best aspects of romantic relationships—devotion, affection, commitment, pleasure, vulnerability, and cherishing one another?

What would it take to treat our friends in the most caring ways we treat our lovers, and our lovers in the best ways we treat our friends?

Nonexclusivity to Expand Our Support and Connections

The romance myth encourages isolation and exclusivity in relationships, and many people seek or demand exclusivity in nonromantic or nonsexual relationships as well. This might, for example, look like experiencing jealousy that your best friend is going on a trip with a new friend. Certainly, we share special activities with certain people, but using exclusivity as the marker of care or significance leads to jealousy, possessiveness, control, and isolation. Exclusivity can look like love in a culture based in scarcity and fear, but it gets in the way of everyone having an abundance of connection.

To thrive, we need more robust, promiscuous emotional support systems. Who do you talk to about your struggles, your explorations, and your good news? Who are your confidants? Who listens to you with compassion, without judgment, and shares your excitement about areas of growth and exploration? If you want to expand this pool, consider who might be the right people in your circles to begin this work with. Who of your friends and lovers have similar values? Who in your orbit might be ripe for more intentional outreach—or who might you spend more one-on-one time with?

Many of us are isolated. Perhaps you've been in an insular relationship or maybe you haven't learned how to make close friends because of conditions like ableism or racism impacting how people treat you. Maybe your family taught you to distrust people or keep relationships shallow. Where can you find friends who might become confidants? At an art class, a reading group, support group, a faith space, a twelve-step meeting, an activist project? Do you want to add more in-person group activities to your life to build more connection? Or do you need to reduce the amount of time and social energy you are spending in some activity or relationship that is impacting your chances of finding friends in new ways?

You might also examine whether you've been pursuing emotional exclusivity, overtly or covertly, with any of your friends or lovers. What could allow you to feel that you and your loved ones are actually safer and more connected if everyone has many sources of support? (See the section on jealousy later in this chapter for more on that.)

Unfortunately, relationships based on principles of mutual liberation are uncommon in our society. For all the reasons described in this book, romantic and sexual relationships are rarely this free. Family relationships are bogged down in prescribed roles, and work and school relationships are often hierarchical and oppressive. From what I have seen, friendship is the closest most people get to each other. This is not to say that people don't mistreat their friends. However, friendship is more likely than those other relationships to include liberating connective practices like giving and receiving honest feedback and wanting what is best for the other person rather than wanting to control them. A society governed by mandated, heavily legislated family relationships and the romance myth has little use for friendship, and generally undervalues it. This makes friendship a refuge for freer relational practices that thrive outside the confines of romantic love and family. Increasing the significance of our friendships leads to more of the liberated connection we need to survive these harrowing times.

* What do you imagine liberated relationships would look like?
* Are there any characteristics of liberated relationships that you are already experiencing, or have felt in the past?
* Where would you add more relational support or connection in your life? Are there certain things you wish to share with someone who truly understands?

Make Your Friends in the Resistance

My greatest hope for everyone who reads this book is that, if you are not already involved, you will join the resistance. I hope you are part of groups working on destroying systems of domination, helping people survive the current crises, and preparing for the catastrophes that are coming. Now, as we face the collapse of consumer industrial society, we desperately need dense networks of support and care. We still depend on unjust systems for our basic needs, and those systems are crumbling. More and more, we will be forced to rely on each other to get by.

When we meet each other through social movement work, we might find that our friends are unlike us in many ways. They might not be in our age group or subculture, or have a similar life history. But shared commitment to resistance is a beautiful basis for deep connection. Rather than a common taste in music or sports, the people we meet in resistance work might share our passion to house unhoused people in our neighborhood, to block a pipeline project, to close down a prison, or to shut down a weapons manufacturer.

Building skills and taking risks together is a profound bedrock for building trust, friendship, and love of all kinds, particularly when our actions are based in shared beliefs about what freedom and liberation means. Of course, we can still get hurt in relationships that emerge in resistance work. But it's my belief that if there's anywhere we can find liberatory ways to relate, it will be when we gather to fight for liberation. My twenty-five years in resistance work has generated relationships that have sustained me in every way, often with people I never would have otherwise met. Knowing how different we were, and yet how mutually committed to shared visions of liberation, strengthened our capacity to engage our differences, overcome false divisions, and learn from and cherish each other.

Allowing, Accepting, or Even Liking Our Differences

TO HAVE THE kind of liberated connections we want, we have to feel how we are both *connected to* and *autonomous from* other people. It's a nuanced and complicated business. Sometimes we feel one or the other of these more strongly than is useful, and it makes our relationships difficult, or even prevents connection altogether. One way to talk about this difficulty is to explore the idea of *codependence*. Much has been written on this, including my note on p. 196 about how this idea can be misused to stigmatize interdependence.

When we blame someone else for how we feel, or when we take responsibility for someone else's feelings, we stunt the growth of the relationship and the people in it. Blaming others for our own feelings often looks like accusing someone else of making us angry, jealous, claustrophobic, or the like. Taking responsibility for someone else's feelings often looks like withholding our own opinions, feelings, plans, or requests because we fear the other person will feel threatened by them.

In codependent relationships, we lose our autonomy; we fear change; we fear letting *others* change. If we fear abandonment, this might look like feeling threatened if the other person changes, wants something new, or relates in new ways with other people. Rather than wishing for the other person to get what they want out of life, we try to rein them in. If we fear engulfment, the codependent dynamic might include being afraid of doing what we want, or even talking about it, because of how it might make the other person feel.

Remember Mustafa, who feared telling his partner that he needed more time alone, because he thought it would upset her? This approach often leads to resentment. Codependency with fear of engulfment can also present as an inability to tolerate the other person's insecurity, or an attempt to control it by giving them advice or shutting them down when they share their fears. It might even include hiding or lying about what we are doing or feeling to avoid upsetting the other person. In these situations, whether feeling fear of abandonment or engulfment, we are suffering from a painful entanglement: we can't stand to let the other person fully be themselves.

When people are experiencing this kind of codependency, they might not say no to each other or ask for things directly. One person might make all the decisions, or the relationship might not allow separate friends or activities. At worst, it might turn into a situation in which the two people have no outside friends, and aren't talking to anyone else about the relationship. Sadly, this kind of insularity jibes with the romance myth's instruction to make our partner our whole world. What feels delightful during an initial stage of wish-fulfillment projection can quickly turn painful, because we suppress one another in order to mask our differences. Paradoxically, our desire to be close leads us to this miserable—if culturally acceptable—relationship style. The truth is, it isn't intimacy if we don't get to be ourselves, if we are struggling to fit ourselves into small containers to keep each other's fears at bay.

Some psychologists believe that our relationships go through developmental stages. Similar to what I described in Chapter Three, they suggest that we start with a *bonding* stage filled with positive projections, of feeling very close and engaging in behavior similar to infant-caregiver bonding. Ideally, relationships then proceed to a *differentiation* stage, in which we reconnect to our separateness and autonomy while remaining connected and caring. As discussed in Chapter Three, as the initial bonding wears off, there is often significant disappointment and conflict about the actual differences between the people, which have been masked or downplayed during the bonding stage. Ideally, that conflict supports emotional growth and can lead people to feel both connected and separate, able to express their needs and limits, accept each other's differences, give and receive feedback, and appreciate one another. This process is called *differentiation*, in which people come to feel their separateness and find it to be a resource, rather than a threat to their connection.

In *Polywise*, Jessica Fern, whose exploration of New Relationships Energy we discussed in Chapter Two, describes how many couples that open their relationships stumble upon their unfinished differentiation work. Starting relationships with other people, and dealing with the logistics that can entail, exposes where a couple has been unknowingly stuck in codependency. She suggests that it is common for relationships to get stuck in the conflict stage that emerges after the initial bonding, in which people are butting up against their differences. Our culture prizes the initial bonding stage of love, telling us that that is the entirety of love and romance. If we internalize these ideas, ordinary differences between people can feel like violations and threats, and it can seem, consciously or unconsciously, like the best option is to try to prevent one another's development and expression. People get stuck trying to reach back into bonding, disappointed in each other's failures to deliver the perfection they projected at the start of the relationship. Couples can also slide into a dynamic where they police each other into behaving in ways they projected or hoped for at different moments in the relationship.

Differentiation requires the work described throughout this book—cultivating emotional awareness, asking for what we want directly, saying yes and no, learning to accept other people's boundaries, realizing we can't get all our needs met by one person. Everything in dominant culture militates against this emotional development work, telling us to numb what we feel and want and to replace our desires with consumer whims and escapist distractions. It tells us to objectify other people, seeing them as the sources of our good feelings and causing us to feel anger when they don't comply with our (often unspoken or unconscious) desires. It tells us to shape ourselves to fit others' visions so we can get love.

Differentiation requires rigorous, rebellious awareness of ourselves and acceptance of others, things that are discouraged by systems that demand compliance. And it requires us to take responsibility for our feelings, not judging ourselves for having them, but also not blaming others for them or following whatever those feelings tell us to do. When our engulfment fears start filling our heads with thoughts like, "I have to get away," "I don't like them anyway," "He is trying to control me," we can learn how to spot the pattern of fear and curtail it before we follow those reactions in ways that disconnect us from the love we want.

When our abandonment fears are telling us to cling and control, when we are being hypervigilant and seeking evidence of how the other person might be leaving us, we can instead spot the pattern and choose our next actions. As we have explored in prior sections, practicing giving and receiving direct feedback and actually listening to each other is a core way to build trust. It is also key to getting to be separate people while also being connected. This is true of any relationship, no matter how intimate.

In the discussion of forgiveness in Chapter Five, we looked at how even when someone is not willing or available to go through a repair process, you can still engage in a forgiveness process. Similarly, we can work on differentiation in any relationship, with any person living or dead, regardless of whether they are working on it. Relationship dynamics require all the people in them to keep them going, so when you change what you're doing, the whole relationship changes.

While it's true that working on our own side of any relationship can help, this is not a reason to stay in a relationship that is not working for you. Trying to do all the work to save a relationship by ourselves does not work. However, doing work on our part of the dynamics—improving our boundaries, giving feedback, saying no and accepting when others say no—can bring significant change. (We can't do other people's work anyway, or force them to do it, so our only option is to look at our side.) I see this frequently with people entangled in codependent family dynamics. Those can be very hard places to say no, to be honest, and to make decisions based on what we want. Oftentimes, family members are uninterested in doing work around self-awareness. However, we can still break with old scripts. When we exit an old dynamic, for example, by saying no to a family member's request, the other person might protest, make accusations and threats, and call us names. Learning how to hold true to ourselves under such pressure can be transformative in that relationship and across our lives.

* Can you recognize the developmental process of bonding and then differentiating in your relationships with friends, family, lovers, collaborators, and groups?
* Can you relate to the feeling of wanting to control someone and stop them from changing, feeling like their expression or development is a threat to your security? What situations have brought that up for you?
* When have you felt like someone else is responsible for your feelings?
* When have you felt like you are responsible for someone else's feelings, like you can't do what you want to do or be yourself because it will upset them?
* Are there any relationships in your life that would benefit from differentiating? Why? How might you go about that?

Generating Our Own Safety and Security

THE US HAS the largest prison system in human history and a growing military budget already bigger than that of 144 countries combined. In the context of racial capitalism and under the influence of the global US empire, we have been taught to seek security through surveillance, punishment, and control.[1] Blame, judgment, and hypervigilance are baked into us ("I need to control other people to be safe") as well as dishonesty and indirectness ("I need to hide from other people's vigilance and blame"). If we are going to liberate ourselves from these structures—both the ones run by governments and corporations and the ones inside our heads—we need a different idea about how to get safety and security. Prison and border abolitionists and anti-war movements propose that we could be safer by taking care of each other, by collaborating, by naming harm and addressing it instead of minimizing or covering for it. True safety comes not from having more cops, walls, and weapons, but from practicing solidarity so that we have each other's backs. We must see people—including those different from us—with compassion, rather than turning them into enemies. Collective action—taking care of people, changing social and cultural norms to make oppressive violence inexcusable, ensuring people don't get isolated—can make us safer. These things are done through mutual aid projects, cultural practices, political education, and organizing to take back land, life, and our means of survival from elite domination.

A military- and police-centered ideology teaches us to look for safety outside ourselves. If something is wrong, we call a cop, a parent, a teacher, or some other authority figure, rather than trying to sort it out ourselves and with peers. Using hierarchies to find safety, especially hierarchies that create and maintain illegitimate authority, is futile. Hierarchies based in illegitimate authority are the cause of all the most dangerous things—pollution, poverty, sexual violence, war, etc. Everywhere, I see this pattern of authority-seeking, even among people who want to get rid of police and militaries. When we are emotionally stirred and in conflict, we often want others to see that we are right. Even if we don't turn to official authority figures, many of us gossip or cancel or drag people on social media because we feel like we'll be safe if and when other people take our side. Or we want an outside facilitator or mediator to become a judge and declare us "in the right," and we are unsatisfied if they won't take on that role. We've been conditioned to look for safety outside.

Given how much of the harm we experience and witness is minimized and ignored, the fantasy of being rescued by an outside authority is very predictable, and understandable. However, the illegitimate systems of authority—the police, the school discipline system, the family policing system—are all relentlessly racist and harmful, causing far more damage than they prevent or address. In our intimate lives, we play out the quest for external safety by expecting other people to make us feel safe, and blaming them when we feel afraid or insecure.

Babies and young children need their caregivers to provide two kinds of safety: a safe haven and a secure base. A safe haven is a person the child can come to when they are scared, who will comfort them, who they know they are safe with. A secure base is a person they can launch from to explore the world, who they can sense delighting in their explorations and practices of autonomy, who they can show their accomplishments and with whom they can share their sense of wonder. Of course, no caregiver can perfectly provide these things. Every caregiver is sometimes inadequately soothing or protective, and sometimes too protective, intervening, or distracted to be the loving witness to a child's exploration. In adulthood, we still crave these kinds of safety. We unconsciously project on new friends and lovers, in the initial phase of the relationship, hoping that they might give us what we needed so badly as children.

It is worth noting that we *can* actually have satisfying experiences of these kinds of safety in adulthood and there is nothing wrong with wanting to feel these things. Have you had a friend or lover who, at one time or another, you could really turn to and get comforted when scared? Have you had a relationship where you felt loved in a way that made you brave about exploring new interests or capacities, enjoying how that person witnessed and praised your learning? Crucially, when we realize we are in a relationship where some of that safety is happening, or where we are hoping it will happen, it can be hard to remember that it will still never be perfect or consistent. Expecting perfection is a precondition for disappointment and conflict. Having been trained to seek our safety from outside ourselves, we set ourselves up to be disappointed, demanding, or to act entitled, unable to accept that other people cannot always provide us with our secure bases or safe havens—often because of their own emotional reactions and needs. But if we can shift to understanding that moments of connected safety are actually *our* experiences, generated by our capacities to connect to others, we can begin to cultivate those feelings of safety and security for ourselves.

For instance, you can get better at communicating with people in your life about what kind of support you need when you are having a hard time; you can tell a loved one how you want them to listen when you share your latest endeavors or adventures. You can also recognize when existing relationships are not well suited to provide the feelings of safety you want, even with feedback and requests, so you can seek out additional relationships to get those needs met.

Building Feelings of Safe Haven and a Secure Base

Activities with others	Activities with yourself
Telling people how you want to be listened to in order to feel really heard.	Journaling. Listening to your own stories and imagining a loving inner parent witnessing an inner child. Paying attention rather than being distracted.
Being encouraged to explore new ideas and activities.	Making lists of interests and goals. Getting excited about them. Taking pictures, writing poems, making collages about them.
Being comforted when you are scared or upset.	Soothing yourself when afraid. Speaking kindly to the scared part of you, as you would to a scared child.
Having someone attune to you— paying attention to how you are feeling and what you need right then.	Attuning to yourself—observing where you are now, not trying to change it, cultivating compassion for yourself right now if you can.
Feeling someone express delight in you, show you how you shine in their eyes.	Expressing delight in yourself. Beaming at yourself, praising, feeling proud.
Sharing rituals that build a feeling of consistency, like coming together and saying goodbye in meaningful ways, celebrating accomplishments, birthdays, significant days of the year.	Having rituals with yourself that represent care, acknowledgment of your accomplishments, and support during hard times, like on anniversaries of losses.

Activities with others	Activities with yourself
Engaging in play together—which means any activity that is just for fun and exploration, not trying to do it perfectly or be competitive or judgmental.	Engage in play with yourself. What are you interested in trying without trying to be the best at it—art, dance, sports, birdwatching, guitar? Look out for signs it is becoming too serious, work, or a source of self-judgment.
Feeling someone turn toward you most of the time, including when in conflict.	Turning toward yourself with compassion, rather than judging or blaming, when having hard feelings or losses or when you have made a mistake.

If the things in the second column either don't make sense to you or sound unappealing, that's okay. While there are a zillion memes about loving ourselves, many of us don't really know what that means and won't get much out of the very shallow take on it that pop culture generally provides. Start by asking if you can show yourself even a *small* increase in care about something practical.

When you are having a hard feeling, do you speak to yourself in a judgmental voice? Can you turn that dismissiveness down a notch or even replace it with something more neutral, saying to yourself something like "you're sad right now"? If you notice that habits with your phone, sleep, or food indicate a lack of care for yourself, can you make a modest adjustment and then try to feel proud of that? Would doing any of the activities in the right column of the chart be easier if you had a buddy to do them with, so you could encourage one another and report back?

When you try the things in the left column, notice if you experience feelings of safety and security. This isn't about going out looking for a friend or lover to become our safe haven and secure base—this is likely a recipe for disappointment. Instead, our aim is to cultivate these feelings within ourselves and with others in relationships. "Safe haven" and "secure base" are names of experiences we can cultivate, not types of people we need to find. Notice when it is working, and remember that when it isn't working, you have the capacity to experiment with new methods and seek out additional connections. If you build the muscle of feeling those things in *any* of your relationships, you will feel them more easily *across* all relationships. You are practicing feeling secure and safe, rather than trying to find a person that will make you feel secure and safe.

Sometimes we miss the mark with each other, even if we were trying to create a secure connection. Ideally, when that happens, both parties can figure out what is going on, and try to meet each other more in the moment next time. But we can't expect someone will always provide what would make us feel safe and secure, and blaming and criticizing them if they don't doesn't help. Other people are not vending machines, built to deliver the experiences and feelings we want. Instead, they are our practice partners for developing our capacities to feel, listen, and relate. When we have more relationships to practice in, we are less likely to inhabit a scarcity mindset and be harsh with any one person who isn't able to meet us in the exact way we had hoped.

* Can you think of any times when you have found a safe haven with someone? How about a secure base?
* Can you think of any ways you have found these with yourself?
* Do you already do some of these activities with others or alone? Are there any you would like to incorporate more?

Signaling Safety by Accepting Each Other's Bids

Relationship researcher John Gottman describes how people in relationships of any kind make *bids* for connection with each other. We make bids when we ask another person for attention, help, affirmation, or other kinds of positive connection. For example, when you are walking with your lover and they point to a tree, you accept their bid by looking where they pointed. When they enter the room and greet you, you accept their bid by putting down your phone and making eye contact with them. When you pay close attention to a story they are telling you, or notice their bags are heavy and offer to help, you are exchanging bids. Gottman's research focuses on marriages, and he found that couples who accept each other's bids, who turn toward each other, stay married longer than those who don't. This bids concept applies to any relationship.

Often, people who spend a lot of time around each other start to ignore each other. You might not respond verbally, or you might not listen closely anymore. This is very common in families and cohabitating couples. When people notice our bids and accept them, it can foster feelings of security, but if people in our lives are missing our bids, we might feel more insecure. If that is happening, we can directly request things that might help, like asking for an agreement to put aside phones when greeting each other, or requesting that a friend or partner ask you about the project you're working on. You can also ask your friends or lovers if you're noticing their bids enough. Tracking what is happening with bids is one way to cultivate connection. Often these small but frequent interactions set the tone for the whole relationship, and are easier to work on than some of the pitched conflict areas that only come up occasionally.

Not All Relationships Are for Everything— Being Here for What's Here

FICTIONS ABOUT ROMANCE—alongside our unconscious attempts to recoup love, safety, and security missing from childhood—set the stage for us to dash each other's hopes. The romance myth sets up an escalator for relationships that suggests that sex should lead to falling in love, committing, living together, marriage, children, or whatever versions exist in a given subculture. Many repeatedly feel disappointed in love, as if romantic partners have misled them by refusing to move up that escalator. Others of us have had the experience of being pressured to move up the escalator by lovers.

We can address this by ditching the assumptions of the relationship escalator. Relationships do not need to escalate in a set sequence in order to be meaningful. They don't even need to escalate at all. Hooking up with someone once can be a wonderful way to experience pleasure, learn about sex, appreciate another person's hotness. Never planning to live with a date does not mean your connection isn't important. The enjoyment of novelty and autonomy that can come with having anonymous sex at a gay bathhouse is not somehow inferior to the cozy comfort of a live-in partner. How we choose to connect with various lovers does not indicate how close or significant the relationship is.

It would be lovely if we could meet each other with a clean slate, with no looming expectations, and figure out whether we are having a quick fuck, becoming friends, becoming lovers who sleep over, becoming friends with benefits, falling in love, becoming life partners, or whatever. It would be great if we could let our dynamic ebb and flow, sometimes closer, sometimes more distant, and see what our lives allow and what we choose to cultivate together. Sadly, before we even meet, the romance myth is cooking up conflicts and misunderstandings that prepare the ground for false hopes and conflict. No matter how casual our meeting place, no matter what we say we're after, there is a likelihood that the romance myth will shape someone's expectations in ways that lead to disappointment. Some things that we can all try that will help include:

1. Don't go along with escalation that you don't want. Saying "no thanks" to unwanted escalating activities early and often is more kind than going along and then ghosting when it feels like too much pressure. Potentially escalating activities you might want to say no to:
   * Sleeping over
   * Meeting friends or going to an event together
   * Meeting family
   * Spending a birthday or holiday together
   * Gift exchange
   * Accompanying someone to something difficult, like a medical appointment or funeral
   * Daytime hangout or adventure
   * Pet names for each other

* More communication (frequency, length) or expectation
  of communication like morning/bedtime texts
* Hanging out more often
* Hanging out after sex

2 Listen to what people say about what they want and
track how they act, too. Talk to a friend about the signals
you are seeing and how to keep your expectations
aligned with reality.

3 Don't assume the signals you are reading align perfectly
with the signals someone intends to send. If you need
clarification, ask.

I can't count the number of friends I have had who, after leaving a serious relationship, say they want to have casual sex but instead enter a new relationship with the first or second person they connect with. Often, this leads to drama. Sometimes this person tells their new date they want to keep it casual, but then proceeds to generate closeness more similar to the yearslong relationship they just left. They begin spending a lot of time together, communicating frequently, integrating the new person into their social life, and other behaviors that signal escalation. The two people form different expectations, one based on what they are saying and the other based on what they are doing.

For some people, escalating relationships can feel involuntary, or even compulsive. The highs of emotional bonding can be irresistible and cultural pressures can be compelling. You might intend to keep it casual, but then find yourself making those next moves toward escalation despite your initial intentions. If you find yourself, again and again, in more serious connections than you intended, or in relationships with people whom you did not mean to start dating, it may be worth giving the dynamic some consideration. What emotional needs are you getting met through escalation? How does that clash with other things you want from relationships and from your life? Talking to friends or a therapist about that internal conflict can help. For some people, the Sex and Love Addicts Anonymous twelve-step program can be useful. The pros: SLAA's tools provide a lot of detailed inquiry into how people experience and chase these highs, and like other twelve-step programs, it is free, peer-based, and widely available, online or in-person. The cons: depending on how you navigate it, the program can contribute to internal narratives of shame and self-pathologization.

When we escalate relationships without meaning to, there can be elements of dishonesty—perhaps the person you are escalating with doesn't understand how you really feel about the relationship, and will later feel betrayed. There is also the danger of feeling obligated in the relationship, if you have escalated a relationship unintentionally. Serially entering and escalating relationships, or staying in relationships we don't want to be in, can cause discord in social and political groups as those relationships blow up. We must learn what we want, align our actions with it, and communicate limits clearly for our own flourishing and for our collective well-being.

While some people escalate when they don't mean to, others say they want more connection in sexual and romantic relationships but unconsciously take actions that block this from happening. This often stems from fear or insecurity. There are so many good reasons to be afraid—for instance, the dating sphere is rife with sexism, racism, ableism, classism, and hatred of fat people and trans people. Many of us are afraid of rejection, of being known intimately, or of experiencing mistreatment. These fears may be conscious or unconscious. But we can become so protective of ourselves that we miss potential pleasurable connections.

I have one friend whose fear of being rejected by cis partners makes him standoffish. He wants any potential cis lover to demonstrate perfect skillfulness about approaching trans people, and he wants them to put themselves out there emotionally before he will do the same. He's quick to dismiss anyone who isn't doing this in the way he wants. That protectiveness narrows the field so much that it impedes his ability to find what he wants. His approach makes sense, given pervasive marginalization and devaluing of trans people. Yet, finding a way to be more open, while caring for himself and having appropriate boundaries, is necessary for him to find the kind of connection he is seeking.

This also comes up when people are narrowly specific about what kind of relationship they want, for example being unwilling to connect with anyone unless it will lead to committed partnership. When we feel more secure in ourselves, we can become more flexible, finding greater enjoyment for what is actually available. Yes, crappy, oppressive dynamics do permeate our dating pools, but as we build our capacity to get safety from within ourselves (and potentially in movements and groups where we find comrades and solidarity in fighting these oppressions), we may find that other people's nonsense cuts less deeply or is easier to walk away from, and that we can explore beyond our fears of being hurt or the romance myth's fantasies of being fulfilled.

* Have you ever experienced disappointment or conflict because of poor communication about where a relationship was heading?
* Have you ever felt pressured to make a relationship more serious than you wanted?
* Have you ever felt misled into thinking a relationship would be more serious and then were let down by the other person? Can you think of ways that those situations could have been different?
* Have you seen in yourself or friends the unintentional or autopilot escalation of a relationship? Have you seen yourself or friends struggle with being open and flexible enough to enjoy whatever kinds of relationships are available?

Being Intentional About Levels of Connection

Bianca wants to continue her fun sexual connection with Jill, not get into a serious relationship. But she knows how this has gone for her in the past. She usually ends up entangled in an emotional relationship even when she doesn't mean to. She is trying to figure out how to have it go differently this time.

Iman has an intense crush on his best friend's boyfriend. He can see that nothing good can come of hooking up—it will either mess up their friendship, ruin his friend's relationship, or leave him suffering from outrageous longing. He wants to figure out how to let go of this crush.

Layla has started dating again after a rough breakup. She has done a lot of reflection about her dating life and wants to make some changes, like no sleepovers within the first month of dating, holding boundaries about safer sex, and limiting how much she looks at dates on social media. She also wants to stop dating anyone who is in the military. Layla lives near a base and has gone out with recruits before. But as someone who is dedicated to ending war and militarism, she knows dating soldiers won't work for her.

IF YOU ARE in a situation like Bianca's, where you want to keep sex casual and avoid activities that might push you over the edge into a bonding stage, writing some casual sex protocols might help. Sex educator Reid Mihalko developed a tool for people seeking casual sex to help avoid having the feelings in the relationship escalate. Casual sex protocols are guidelines we can put in place for ourselves to avoid "imprinting" on a new person or "flipping the 'you're dreamy' switch." Reid suggests being intentional about how often you reach out to initiate communication and sex, resisting sleepovers or weekends together. He also offers the idea of exploring group sex, if it's an option, in order to diffuse focused attention on one person. Reid also recommends practicing safer sex, communicating clearly with lovers about your availability and intentions, not gossiping about who you sleep with, and thanking a person after casual sex. His protocols identify what leads to emotional escalation for him, and how he practices boundaries when he does not want to escalate.[2] They might not be the same protocols you would use, but they are useful for inspiration.

Write Your Own Casual Sex Protocols

If you are trying to keep sex casual but know you tend to end up more entangled than you intend, or mislead people about your availability, it can be helpful to write your own casual sex protocols.

Why do you want to keep sex casual, and what could help? Make notes under each category below for potential protocols. Remember, it's not just about saying to yourself or others that you want to keep it casual, but also matching your behavior to your intentions. It can help to write boundaries for certain people, or in general. Make notes about each category.

* Frequency of Dates
* Frequency of Communication between Dates
* Length of Dates
* What You Share About Yourself or Ask About Them
* How You (Do/Don't) Include Them in Your Life

What else would help you follow through with your intention to keep sex casual? What has escalated your connections in the past that you want to avoid this time?

If you are like Iman, with an unwanted crush, it can be useful to consider whether you are stoking the fires of this infatuation. Like everything in life, crushes are a practice. Sometimes that practice is unconscious, and we tell ourselves the crush is happening *to* us, ignore what we are doing to inflame it. When I am stoking a crush, I might listen to songs that make me think about my desire for that person, or the ways I hope we will connect. I might cultivate extra thinking about them, perhaps remembering times we have spent together. I might pursue extra communication with them or go to places where I hope to run into them. So, if I want to tone down my crush feelings, I need to curtail these practices as much as possible. On p. 119, you'll find a tool called Seven Steps for De-Escalating a Crush that may be helpful.

If you are like Layla, and you are figuring out what has not historically worked for you when it comes to dating, a *dating plan* can help you be more intentional about your actions. A dating plan includes anything you want to work on: length of dates, frequency, qualities you are looking for, sex practices to seek or avoid, guidelines for interacting with your dates' online lives, things about yourself you want to show or keep private, methods for getting support from friends about dating, boundaries about how you will keep your own or others' confidences. You can share your dating plan with a friend or therapist and ask them to check in with you about how it is going, but for many people, even just making a dating plan helps bring clarity and greater ease of holding boundaries.

Creating a Dating Plan

If you are noticing what doesn't work in your dating, use that knowledge—particularly your complaints and regrets—to make a plan. The plan is an ongoing experiment: you can try new things as you learn more. It can also include things tangentially related to dating, like the way going on dates affects your sleep, eating, work, friendships, art practice, etc.

These are only prompts; take only what resonates. Your guidelines should be personal to you, based on your experiences and what you know about your patterns.

* Getting support as you use your dating plan, for example:
    * I'll have an honest check-in with a close friend once a week and/or after each date.
* Choosing who to date, for example:
    * I will not date/hook up with anyone if I'd need to mislead, mischaracterize it, or keep it secret from my friends.
    * I will not date/hook up with anyone who is cheating on someone else.
    * I will not pursue anyone who shows signs of being unavailable, like canceling plans frequently or not responding to messages.

* Sharing about yourself and getting to know the other
  person, for example:
    * I will pay attention to the person's cues about whether
      they are actually available for what I am seeking.
    * I will make a list of what I actually know about this
      person if I notice excessive projections, and will talk
      this through with a friend to get a reality check.
    * I will check whether I am being honest about what
      I want when I talk to them, and go back and correct
      anything that has been misleading.
    * I will not rush to share about my healing process,
      my past trauma, or details of my past relationships.
    * I will not look at this person's social media more than
      once every two weeks.
* Making plans about sex (or BDSM/kink, for example):
    * I will initiate and ask for physical contact and sex when
      I want it, rather than always waiting to be asked.
    * I will wait to engage in power exchange until I have
      had a conversation establishing clear limits.
    * I will not include bondage in sex with this person
      while either of us is intoxicated.
    * I will not have sex that puts my health at risk in the
      ways that have been a repeated pattern in the past.

Another approach to this kind of boundary setting with yourself is to make a list of *bottom lines*—things you are absolutely committed to do or not do—about dating. Examples of bottom lines might include:

* I will follow my safer sex protocols with all my dates.
* I will sleep at home the nights before my 8-a.m. class.
* I will not drink more than two drinks on a date.

These bottom lines are just examples—every person will have different ones they find useful. You can also make a list of *top lines*—things you know would be supportive to what you want and that you will do when you can. Top lines might include:

* I will plan an exciting date with my best friend twice a month, making sure I don't only put that date energy into my crush.
* I will spend one weekend afternoon in nature by myself.
* When I feel protective and judgmental, I will try to stay open to the possibility of connection with people who approach me.

All of these tools are ways to get clearer about what we want and don't want and to execute those choices more intentionally. Even simply exploring the tools can build our sense of safety and security in ourselves.

❓

* Have you been in any of the situations that Layla, Iman,
  or Bianca are in? How did you handle them?
* Have you tried using boundaries, like bottom lines, to
  address dating situations? What happened?
* Could talking to someone else about your efforts help?
  If so, who would you choose to talk to and why?

Setting Your Bottom Lines

What are two realistic bottom line commitments you can
make right now that you know will bring more of what
you want in life? Pick something that you can actually
do, rather than something that might set you up to feel
more disappointment or shame. Here are a few areas of
behavior where you might look for a bottom line:

* Relationship to sex and
  dating apps or to your
  phone in general
* Bedtime and supporting
  good sleep
* Length, frequency, or
  type of dates

* Relationship to using
  intoxicants on dates
* Taking care of health needs
* Safer sex
* Eating enough and
  drinking enough water

Establishing bottom lines, telling a friend or suppor
person about them, and celebrating successf
of keeping your commitments can help move y
internal trust and security.

Jealousy

Kenneth just got a new job at an art gallery. He's so excited. He gets to meet interesting artists and tons of people who come to openings or host events in the space. His world is suddenly opening up, connecting with new friends who have shared interests. His boyfriend, Haoran, was enthusiastic and supportive at first, but now he's jealous that Kenneth is gone so many evenings and talking about all the interesting people he is meeting.

Haoran isn't in the art world and worries these people are out of his league. He is cranky with Kenneth, saying rude or dismissive things about the people or events Kenneth describes. When Kenneth invites him along, he feels uncool and awkward when Kenneth is talking with other people. Haoran worries he's a bad person for not being more happy for Kenneth.

Jealousy is common in all kinds of relationships. For some people, jealousy includes a lot of comparing oneself to another person, fearing that they are smarter, sexier, or somehow better. Others focus less on the other person and more on the fear of change or loss in the existing relationship. Jealousy can lead to behavior that strongly departs from our values, like blowing up, unfairly criticizing, trying to control others, trying to sabotage connections, and/or violating people's privacy.

In this book, I encourage emotional and relational promiscuity—I believe we should get our needs met from many relationships. When we are jealous, it is hard to keep sight of a commitment to generous, open relationships that value autonomy. Jealousy orients us outward, blaming others, shaming others, or wanting to lash out. The path to deep connection and emotional safety is through awareness of our patterns of feeling and behavior, especially when our feelings are heightened and we want to blame or control others. We need strong, cohesive networks of connection in our lives to weather the storms that are here and coming, and to undergird our collective efforts at liberation.

This book is about turning inward toward our emotions, so we can make decisions about the life we build in community. Jealousy, exclusivity, and control are aligned with a culture of policing, punishment, war, private property, individualism, and surveillance. Our liberation practices seek collectivity, mutuality, care, forgiveness, generosity, and acceptance.

Jealousy is exacerbated by the shame we experience in its thrall. We might try to hide it, which can make it more explosive in the long run. Shame can also lead us to defend and rationalize our jealousy, because we dislike admitting that we're having a feeling we wish we did not have. Unfortunately, shame and denial don't work. Turning *toward* our hardest feelings with love and compassion, as much as possible, can prevent them from running our lives.

When I am gripped by jealousy, I try to think that there is a scared child inside me, and I say calming, neutral things to them, like, "You're scared right now." I don't try to talk them out of the feeling; I just try to remind that part of me that the emotion will eventually pass. Jealousy says, "This is intolerable, I can't stand this." But like all emotions, jealousy arises and then passes away.

Even if I am having days or weeks of jealousy, it won't be at its worst all the time, and there will be periods of being distracted from it. Even reminding ourselves that it is temporary is a massive shift from its message of "THIS IS INTOLERABLE! DO SOMETHING!!," which often points us outward toward blaming and controlling, or distancing and departing.

We can also avoid shaming ourselves if we give space to that jealous part of us that needs compassion. We don't need to stifle our jealous feelings—and trying through force of will to overcome jealousy simply doesn't work. Having jealous feelings doesn't hurt others or violate our principles; it's just part of life.

It's only when we turn our jealousy outward—through control, blame, judgment, or violating others' privacy—that we cause hurt and violate our principles. These jealous feelings are reasonable responses to what we've been through in life and the conditions in which we were raised. The aim is to ensure our actions line up with our principles and desires.

Many of us get emotionally stirred up when someone we love feels jealous toward something we are doing. We might feel accused, or afraid that something we have done is wrong, or that someone is trying to control us. It is common, and even reasonable, to be hurt or defensive in the face of jealousy. But just as the jealous person, ideally, soothes the small, scared person inside, so too should the person who is the object of jealousy.

Rather than acting out of defensiveness, we can start by having compassion for ourselves, for how scared we feel of being controlled or accused, for how disappointed we are that the other person can't delight in our exploration of the world. For some of us, our fear of stirring jealousy can prompt us to hide things or lie to a lover or friend—it's important to attend to our own scared selves in order to avoid the dishonesty that can undermine any relationship. We can often defuse a difficult moment's worst aspects if we say to each other: "These are challenging feelings, but here is how I want to keep being kind to myself and to you."

We can ask each other for specific kinds of support and reassurance, though someone might or might not be able to deliver that help. When we are in a jealous state, do we want touch? Reassuring words? Time alone? When jealousy is stirred up in me, I have learned it's better not to discuss the specific cause or content of the jealousy, because I'm likely to say something that I will regret. My deep wish is to have everyone in my life do what will bring them pleasure, connection, belonging, and the full expression of their creativity. When I am jealous, I don't want to speak in a barbed, critical way that might undermine those deeply held principles. Instead, I want to connect and get comfort, without needlessly being unkind.

I have sometimes given the other person a few ideas ahead of time of what will help most—how I want to be touched or what words I might find soothing if jealousy arises—as I'm unlikely to be able to ask for those things when actively feeling insecure. Making those requests does not mean the other person can always fulfill them. Such a request can't be a demand, nor can difficulty fulfilling it be the basis for criticism. My hope is that people I feel jealousy around can come to see that it has nothing to do with them or anything they did, but rather is like a lingering feeling, as if I'm waking from a bad dream. Childhood experiences and cultural scripts have planted reactions in me that I know don't match reality. My goal is to ask for my loved one's patience as I continue the slow process of learning how to feel safe and secure.

* Have you ever blamed or controlled other people to try to deal with jealousy? Is there anything you were once jealous about that has now changed?
* Have you experienced jealousy arising and then passing away?

* Have you ever hidden something to control someone else's jealousy?
* Could you imagine being able to hear about jealousy and not think it was your fault? What would it take to feel that?

///

///

Mad Mapping Jealousy

Are there things you want to make sure you don't say or do when you are in the grips of jealousy? A mad map can be a little gift of preparation for a future self who is headed into potentially stormy emotional waters. This version is geared toward jealousy, but feel free to adapt it for any strong emotional state. Your mad map could have any areas or categories, could be illustrated or include songs or physical movements. Below are some starter ideas and examples of potential content.

Distorted thinking and feeling that comes up when I am jealous, examples of which could include:

* Thinking the other person has done something wrong
* Thinking negative things about the other people or about situations that relate to the jealousy
* Wanting bad things to happen to other people
* Feeling punitive or vengeful
* Feeling low/dejected and obsessively waiting for communication from them
* Feeling like I can't ask for reassurance

* Feeling insatiable—no reassurance is enough
* Acting like the other person is dishonest or not trustworthy when they haven't done anything to deserve that
* Thinking badly of myself, comparing and despairing
* Feeling shame about my feelings, wanting to hide or get away
* Feeling like the feelings of jealousy are intolerable, not being able to remember that they will end
* Coming up with controlling requests or demands in hopes they will make me feel better (they won't)

Sobering realities to remember. Examples could include:

* I want the other people to have good experiences, connection, care, and pleasure.
* I am safe. Other people's connections and pursuits don't actually threaten my well-being.
* These feelings will pass. I don't always feel this way.
* I am choosing the things in my life.
* I want my own liberation, which means letting these feelings pass through me without dictating my action.
* I can ask for support from friends, connect with pets or nature, rest, distract myself, move my body, or use other methods to get through this difficult moment.

Where this has led before that I want to avoid?
Examples could include:

* Saying unkind things to others
* Making controlling or manipulative demands
* Being dishonest
* Violating other people's privacy
* Doing things that further stir the jealousy, like looking
  at certain people on social media or playing back scenes
  in my head
* Picking fights
* Reaching for distractions or highs that will make me feel
  worse in the long run
* Not asking for help that I need

Things I could do to get a little more in touch with
reality, examples of which could include:

* Take a pause from communicating with the person I am
  feeling jealous about or from checking for messages from
  them—bring my focus to something else
* Hang out with a friend who will understand
* Read a book about jealousy that has helpful or soothing
  ideas
* Engage with something about nature, spirituality, time,
  space, or anything that draws me back into a broader
  perspective

* Reread a list I've made (add to this mad map!) of my
  principles regarding liberation and wanting the best
  for others, and the reasons I want to live by them
  (for myself and my own pleasure and wellness)
* Remember (if I can) the kind and generous things the
  other person does for me

    You could also include other elements on this map,
such as:
* Music I should/shouldn't listen to right now (music that
  stirs romance myth ideas may not be helpful now)
* Physical activities that help move the energy through
  me or bring calm or connection to self
* Activities that connect me to nature, art, or spirit that
  could support me in finding balance in myself
* Limits or boundaries with internet or social media
* Breathing exercises
* Guided meditations
* Writing a letter to the scared part of me
* Visualizing myself holding a scared child that represents
  the jealous part of me; speaking soothing phrases that
  don't negate its feelings; for example: "you're scared
  right now"

What We Can Ask of Others When
We Are Jealous

Zeena and Ahmad have been together for five years and recently opened their relationship. They are both nervous but also excited, and can already feel how this is enlivening their sex life together, as well as reconnecting them to their commitments with each other. They love to do partner dancing together, and Ahmad feels jealous when he thinks about Zeena meeting other people at those events or dancing with people she is hooking up with. He has asked her to not hook up with people she meets dancing, and not dance with her other dates.

Sometimes we want to get safe by asking people to stop doing the things that make us feel jealous. We think these stipulations will make us less jealous, even if they won't. Jealousy tells us that the problem is coming from what others are doing. Demands like these actually undermine our connections because they involve controlling others—and they can strengthen jealousy's grip on us. I've become concerned about how much of the literature on nonmonogamy includes lists of agreements that incorporate these kinds of external-facing efforts at control. Many nonmonogamy resources list things like: agreeing not to have sex on a first date with others, agreeing not to do certain sexual acts with others, or agreeing not to see or communicate with other dates too often. We must recognize that our lovers' connections to others are not actually a threat to our safety, even though scared parts of us sometimes feel that way. Controlling other people's connections is not a legitimate emotional need.

At the same time, it makes sense that people might negotiate pacing when they are changing a relationship to include more or deeper connections with others. Examining urgency is a useful way to build emotional awareness. Perhaps someone is rushing the transition to nonmonogamy—the person might want to speed toward someone they desire, or they're afraid they'll miss their chance for sex or romance with a new person. There's no exact science for how to approach these difficult situations, but all efforts should begin by taking responsibility for our own feelings, considering others', and honoring each person's fears and autonomy.

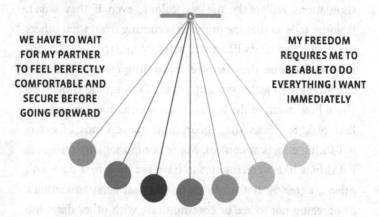

WE HAVE TO WAIT FOR MY PARTNER TO FEEL PERFECTLY COMFORTABLE AND SECURE BEFORE GOING FORWARD

MY FREEDOM REQUIRES ME TO BE ABLE TO DO EVERYTHING I WANT IMMEDIATELY

Many people get stuck on one or the other side of this pendulum, or are fighting between these two sides: wanting the other to feel safe from abandonment or wanting to feel safe to explore. If you are stuck fighting for either position, check for either fear of abandonment or fear of engulfment—and examine the results honestly. Can you attend to those fears rather than getting lost in the content of the fight? Are you blaming someone else for your fears or demanding that they resolve them for you? What can help you remember that you are choosing this relationship? When afraid, we often lose sight of choice, because we feel we are under existential threat of abandonment or engulfment. The truth is this: we are in a consensual relationship. We get to work together to try to find a way to get what we want in life that we can both live with. If we can't find a path, that might be an indicator that it is time to break up.

Finding that path through strong feelings—offering care rather than changing each other's behavior or controlling each other—works out better in the long run. Exploring fears about someone else's autonomous exploration or feelings of jealousy can build intimacy where, unaddressed, those fears can cause disconnection. True safety cannot come through controlling a loved one's authentic feelings or actions.

Some people feel that open relationships are inherently more insecure than monogamous ones, that by connecting with more people we open the door to possible loss or change.

But a monogamous relationship can also end or change at any time. People can (and do) feel strong jealousy even in monogamous relationships. While nonmonogamous relationships are not inherently more insecure, they do require more differentiation than monogamous relationships, because we acknowledge our separateness when we openly pursue sexual and/or romantic connections with others.[3]

As I said earlier, there is no politically superior relationship type. Similarly, there is no relationship mode that is better for shaking off the cultural baggage and childhood shaping we struggle with; we can do that work anywhere in our lives, and we must. Nonmonogamy might reveal codependency and reliance on the romance myth that could have been hidden previously in a monogamous relationship. There is nothing wrong with choosing any relationship style, yet it's useful to notice if we lean on one style to avoid our fears of abandonment or engulfment—particularly if that avoidance is squeezing our life too tight. We can connect to principles of liberation in *all* our relationships, sexual and nonsexual, and cultivate genuine desire for the freedom and well-being of all people alongside tender care for the scared parts of us and our beloveds. We are all trying to connect and have fun and get love under the influence of powerful, culturally permeated scripts. It is a big undertaking, requiring patience and practice.

* Can you think of requests you've made based on the idea that controlling the other person's actions could resolve your jealousy or make you emotionally safer?
* Can you think of requests for support you've made when feeling jealous that *didn't* rely on controlling someone else's actions?
* How might examining your own urgency give you more patience with people when they are having strong feelings?

Love Changes You

People turn their lives upside down for love. Love can be immensely motivating. This can be beautiful. I have seen friends rediscover their creativity, their sexual expression, or their passion for justice because of a new sexual or romantic relationship. It can also be awful. I have known people whose new relationship became a place where they lost self-esteem, became isolated, or turned away from their values in order to bond with a lover who felt threatened by their other activities or relationships. People blossom, take on whole new identities, or cut out vital parts of themselves under the influence of lovers. There is no doubt that love can change us, deeply.

Love is dangerous and full of liberatory potential because of the ways that it can shake us loose from what we are doing, can help us desire new horizons and shift to meet them. How do you want to be changed by love? What about you and your life do you want to protect from being lost or changed by love?

Accepting Change

IT'S HARD TO accept the truth that people and relationships always change. The romance myth insists that change is a betrayal, that we should punish people into loving us the way we want, and that change means something is wrong. In this way, relationships of all kinds, but especially family and romantic relationships, become sites of confinement. We blame others for changing and blow up at them or stonewall them. We fear others' feelings, so we limit our growth and experimentation or lie about it.

The path through all this is awareness of our own emotions and a commitment to principles of liberation. We can practice building security with ourselves and our support system that will hold us even if someone else disappears, lies to us, or tries to control us, because we know we will take care of ourselves and be held by the many people who love us. We don't need others to be perfect for us to be safe: we generate that safety by building our own awareness of what we want and need and our ability to communicate it to others. We know how to say (and hear) yes and no. We don't keep all our eggs in one person's emotional basket, even if we feel intensely connected to them.

We can feel the vulnerability that strong attachments stir up, and savor the chance to treat ourselves and others with care. When we accept that change is inevitable, we get to worry less about being lied to or controlled. When we know that everyone has strong emotional reactions to relating, we can lovingly witness those reactions in ourselves and others without shaming or blaming, and without letting those reactions control our actions.

Once, when I was struggling with a particularly painful relationship drama, a friend described how she sometimes saw herself in such moments. She imagined herself as a person with two bodies, connected at the back. One was pulling her, desperate and clingy, toward her lover. The other was dragging her away. This image stuck with me—how, when things are hard, we feel simultaneously that we desperately need to be with another person and that we can't stand to be around them. At times I've thought I was "bad at intimacy" when I was having these issues, particularly when I was feeling the avoidant part.

What I've learned, though, is that we all get scared in relationships. Intimate relationships stimulate our core desires for belonging, connection, safety, and creative expression. We want and need each other so badly, and that means we stir each other deeply. At best, we can cultivate our relationships as laboratories where we study, experiment, and practice learning about ourselves and unearthing cultural scripts we want to break ties with. To build new social relations based on mutuality, care, collectivity, and generosity, we need to practice new things, all the time, with all the people around us. We need radical emotional and relational promiscuity, so that we can survive and resist together.

Chapter Six Recap

* The romance myth encourages isolation and exclusivity, which strangles our relationships and deprives us of the robust support systems we all need.
* Codependency, where we blame someone else for our feelings or take responsibility for someone else's feelings, causes relationships to get stuck in resentment and conflict. In codependent relationships, we feel threatened by someone else changing or growing or being different from us.
* Differentiation is when people in a relationship accept that they have different needs and preferences rather

than resisting or resenting those differences. It requires learning: to ask for what we want, to accept other people saying no, and to give and receive direct feedback.

* We're trained in a punishment-centered culture to seek safety from outside ourselves. This can make us resent loved ones for anything they do that stirs up our fears. Important aspects of safety and security actually come from inside us, however. They are emotional capacities we can build by learning to say no, asking for what we want, and noticing when we are being supported.

* Romance myth expectations about how relationships should escalate cause a great deal of conflict. Because those expectations are common, we need to be intentional when we communicate about what we want with someone, and try to align our actions with our words.

* Jealousy is damaging to relationships when we point it outward at our loved ones, blaming them for our feelings, trying to control them, or violating their privacy. Working with our jealousy by being kind to ourselves when experiencing those feelings can help. Trying to stop our feelings by controlling others' actions does not.

conclusion: We're in This Together

> The only lasting truth is change.
> —OCTAVIA BUTLER, *Parable of the Sower*

> We are the ones we have been waiting for.
> —JUNE JORDAN, *"Poem for South African Women,"*
> *from* Passion *(1980)*

MANY OF US turn toward self-help tools with the hopes of instantaneous change. Capitalism sells promises of total health, wealth, and blissful happiness. But in reality, being alive is a wild, constantly changing mix of beauty, suffering, agony, contentment, and dissatisfaction. No matter how we fight it, everything around us is impermanent. Everything we want and love will come to an end, just as our lives will.

We have to approach both our relationships with other people and our own healing with a humble outlook and reasonable expectations. One question often guides me when I am stuck: "What am I so afraid of being seen doing that I am willing to limit my steps toward what I want in life?"[1]

If you use the methods outlined in this book, you might experience more emotional awareness. You might begin to notice the moments when you are gripped by autopilot reactions. You might hear cultural scripts—like the romance myth norms or scarcity thinking—running through your mind and find ways to resist their pull. You might be able to think "that's not me, that's not mine." You might notice when you are reacting in ways that are out of proportion to the situation. Perhaps you might connect this reaction to a fear of abandonment or engulfment, and recover before you say or do something hurtful to someone you love. Or you might say those hurtful things but be better able to apologize. You might gossip less. You might find your conflicts bring you closer to others rather than damaging your relationships with them.

You might become better able to say "yes," "no," and "maybe" to other people. You might find that autopilot reactions still arise in you, but they don't determine your behavior and you recover more quickly. You might not feel as much shame about them. You might find that people or situations that used to really get under your skin just don't get you as worked up anymore.

It has helped me to return to the phrase I mentioned earlier: "healing is a spiral staircase." I think about myself walking a circle, like a clock. As I heal, I will reencounter, again and again, the wounds that have shaped my life and the coping mechanisms I developed to get through rough times.

Each time I reencounter them, rather than being ashamed to still be affected or disappointed that I'm not "fixed" yet, I try to cultivate acceptance. This is the hand I was dealt. And everything in my life—all that is beautiful and all that is rough, all that is shared and all that is lonely—stems from this same hand.

My task is to cultivate discernment and clarity about these conditions so that I can act with compassion and intention, rather than being blown around by the cultural forces that try to shape me and a past I can't change. I can be grateful for the coping mechanisms I came up with as a kid, and also decide to update how I react to the world around me, to develop habits and foster choices that get me more of what I want and better align with my values and beliefs. I also have to remember that I am not something to be improved—there is no "fixing"— even as I seek to cultivate new skills and capacities.

Life is not going to get easier in the years to come—the crises we are facing are real and worsening. Most of us are in some denial about this, because it is overwhelming, hard to comprehend. Reports of global heating, mass extinctions, sea level rise, extreme weather, failing crops, ocean acidification, zoonotic diseases, deforestation, and melting ice sheets have become more dire than scientists had predicted even just a few years ago. The industrial consumer society that created this crisis has already caused such irreversible damage to the planet that our lives will certainly be irrevocably altered.

Many people are already acutely affected. Even if all governments in the world stopped pandering to the interests of the ultrawealthy and even if all industries immediately stopped polluting (neither of which is likely to happen), the damage already inflicted is irreversibly changing the planet.

We can, and should, try to reduce any harm that we can, but we also have to face the reality that our lives are about to get much harder.[2] Contemporary human society is dependent on extractive systems for survival—the way we eat, travel, get health care and communicate all pollutes and extracts, and the Covid pandemic revealed the fragility of the supply chains that keep this situation afloat.

It's all so bad, and it's about to get so, so much worse. Even those of us who understand the degree to which ecological crisis is already killing and displacing tens of millions of people (let alone other species) annually are mostly missing the scale of the impending global collapse. It's not just decades of media refusal to adequately cover the crisis, or conspiracies by polluting industries designed to mislead us. We are also lulled into complacency by self-serving politicians and nonprofits overselling the promise of wildly insufficient policy reforms and bullshit tech solutions.

Even as this previously preventable collapse unfolds, we have been misled about how dire things are. We have been led to believe that governments and experts will fix this. The catastrophic impacts are multiplying, yet we are fed feel-good stories about renewables and urged to funnel our profound fears and desires for collective action into individual consumer choices, social media posts, voting, and donating to nonprofits whose efforts at policy reform only tinker with the overarching systems causing the crisis.

This is the reality of our situation, and in the times to come, we are going to need each other more than ever. As I work to let this incomprehensible and heartbreaking truth into my life, I am filled with anger and grief. But hand in hand with that grief is an even deeper appreciation for the beauty of the living planet and the bold resistance and care that people demonstrate every day in the face of these conditions. I am inspired to further divest from the systems of greed that have created this mess, and to shake off all the bad ideas and habits they have implanted in my psyche.

I ask myself: how do I want to be in these times? Again and again, the answer I come to is that I want to face up to these tragedies with an open and loving heart. I want to be part of collective efforts to care for others and stop as much destruction as possible. I want to appreciate every remaining moment of my life, even knowing that much is out of my control. I want to live according to my principles and priorities, not wasting time on nonsense I've been told is important. I want to be deeply connected to the people I love. I want to find more ways to care for strangers and create survival strategies that are collective and inclusive, not distrustful or insular.

In the times to come, we are going to have to find ways to be with one another under enormous stress and in times of devastating grief. We will be called on to demonstrate capacities that are devalued and underdeveloped in dominant society: generosity, courage, connection, compassion, and imagination. I want us to be as awake to what is happening as possible, as capable as we can be to respond in ways that align with collective liberation. I want us to be able to relate to others with as much integrity and compassion as possible, responding to immediate conditions rather than being stuck in old cultural scripts or coping mechanisms that undermine effective action.

The romance myth is a lie. There is no happily-ever-after coming. There never was. Instead, there is the possibility of being here for what's here. Of treating others and ourselves as well as we can. Of experiencing the thrills available in intimacy, collaboration, collective resistance, and belonging. Let's be here for what is here, together, in this gorgeous, fucked-up world.

acknowledgments

SO MANY PEOPLE have been part of generating this book, during both the last nine years that I have been writing it and the prior years of learning about the relational dynamics explored here. It is a pleasure to remember the many coconspirators I have worked side by side with on difficult, joyful, sometimes hare-brained schemes for liberation, together facing the challenges of loving each other through it all. In times like these (or maybe all the time), it's better not to make lists of all our friends and associations, so I'll trust that you know who you are.

Thank you to each person who read drafts of parts of this book and gave me feedback over many years, who recommended books to read, who wrote texts that changed my thinking, and who told me stories that expanded my understanding. Thank you to my teachers, friends, lovers, students, family members, housemates, critics, those who I have collaborated with closely and those who I've joined with temporarily in various efforts—all of you who have shown me what it means to relate, to stick together, and to separate when we need to.

Thank you to those who helped me craft and streamline this manuscript, especially the people who helped me cut 40,000 words in February 2024. I believe that any idea can be made simple, that the most vital and life-changing interventions should feel like liberating common sense when we come upon them, like they were already a part of us. Your thoughtful suggestions made that simplicity much more possible for this book.

The Caldera, Shandaken, and Headlands Artist in Residence programs, and numerous friends, provided much appreciated space and time for developing these ideas.

My literary agent and friend, Rebecca Friedman, believed in this project and found the right launching pad for it. My editor, Evan Hansen-Bundy, enthusiastically engaged in that generative back-and-forth process, making the book so much better than I could alone; what a pleasure, to learn these ideas again, and more deeply, by working them through with you. Thank you to Chris Stamey, Ben Denzer, Cathy Schott, Steve Godwin, and Brunson Hoole for your work editing and designing this book. Books don't get made through magic alone, and I am grateful to all the people whose names I don't know who produce, assemble, and transport the materials that make this book to reach its readers. Thank you to every person keeping libraries, books-to-prisoners projects, and independent and collective bookstores alive. May this book be of service to those working to liberate us all from wage labor, war, pollution, and domination of all kinds.

The Fireweed Collective hosted Valentine's Day webinars four years in a row (2021–24), inviting me to share elements from this book and providing ASL, captioning, and Spanish interpretation. Since I wasn't generally presenting the concepts in these chapters to audiences throughout the nine years of writing, these webinars were essential opportunities to develop the ideas and receive feedback from a community I trust and have much to learn from. I am grateful.

Thanks to the Marguerite Casey Foundation for purchasing over a thousand copies for me to distribute to people in prison.

This book benefits from long lineages of disability-justice, feminist, police- and prison-abolitionist, anarchist, anti-racist, anti-colonial, queer and trans, harm-reduction, and pro-sex social practices, organizing, and writing. I am indebted to the people who, generously and often at great risk, have created and are creating the subcultures, spaces, parties, grief circles, art projects, zines, rituals, books, conversations, and encounters in those lineages.

notes

Introduction

1 Sue Johnson, *Hold Me Tight: Seven Conversations for a Lifetime of Love* (New York, NY: Little Brown Spark, 2008), 15.

2 Ibid., 27. And see Ana Swanson, "What Men and Women Wanted in a Spouse in 1939—and How Different It Is Today," *Washington Post*, April 19, 2016, https://www.washingtonpost.com/news/wonk/wp/2016 /04/19/what-men-and-women-wanted-in-a-spouse-in-1939-and-how -different-it-is-today/.

Chapter One: Dominant Culture's Scripts Are Still Shaping Our Relationships

1 From "Happy Birthday, Marsha," Tourmaline and Sasha Wortzel (2017: New York, NY, video).

2 Of course, people have been challenging these norms forever. I am referring here to a particular wave of resistance that led to the specific recuperation projects of the decades that followed.

3 Political debates about welfare benefits in the US, for example, have been rife with racist, sexist ideas about how Black women and women of color have too many kids and need to get married. This has resulted in federal laws that deny benefits to women who are understood to have "too many" kids, or that put incentives in place for people to marry. The cultural pressure for everyone to get locked down into the state institution of marriage is particularly coercive toward women of color and stigmatizes them and their kids more than it does white women and children. To learn more about this, I recommend the writing of Priya Kandaswamy, Kaaryn Gustafson, Gwendolyn Mink, and Rose Ernst.

4 Conrad, Ryan, *Against Equality: Queer Liberation, Not Mere Inclusion* (Chico, CA: AK Press, 2014) and Dean Spade and Craig Willse,

"Marriage Will Never Set Us Free," *Convergence Magazine*, September 6, 2013. https://convergencemag.com/articles/marriage-will-never-set-us -free/.

5 Johnson, *Hold Me Tight*, 15.

6 Ibid., 24.

7 Johann Hari, *Lost Connections: Uncovering the Real Causes of Depression—and the Unexpected Solutions* (New York, NY: Bloomsbury USA, 2018), 97: "The more kids valued getting things and being seen as having things, the more likely they were to be suffering from depression and anxiety," citing Tim Kasser, *The High Price of Materialism* (Cambridge: MIT press, 2003), 6–8, and Kasser and Ryan, "A Dark Side of the American Dream: Correlates of Financial Success as a Central Life Aspiration," *Journal of Personality and Social Psychology* 65, no. 2 (1993): 410422; Hari at 95–6. "Twenty-two different studies have, in the years since, found that the more materialistic and extrinsically motivated you become, the more depressed you will be. Twelve different studies found that the more materialistic and extrinsically motivated you become, the more anxious you will be"; citing Helga Dittmar et al., "The Relationship between Materialism and Personal Well-Being: A Meta-Analysis," *Journal of Personality and Social Psychology* 107, no. 5 (Nov. 2014): 879–924; Kasser, *High Price of Materialism*, 21.

8 Hari, *Lost Connections*, 97, citing Sherry Turkle, *Reclaiming Conversation: The Power of Talk in a Digital Age* (New York, NY: Penguin, 2015), 83.

9 Cecile Andrews, *Slow Is Beautiful: New Visions of Community, Leisure and Joie de Vivre* (Gabriola Island, B.C.: New Society Publishing, 2006), 16.

10 Andrews, *Slow*, 37, citing Peter Whybrow, *American Mania: When More Is Not Enough* (New York, NY: W. W. Norton and Co., 2005).

11 Jessica Dickler, "Who Wants to Be a Billionaire? 6 in 10 Americans Strive to Be Mega-Wealthy, Report Finds," *CNBC*, August 31, 2022, https://www.cnbc.com/2022/08/31/44percent-of-americans-think-they -can-achieve-billionaire-status.html.

12 Julie Ryan Evans, "Most Gen Zers and Millennials Who Don't

Consider Themselves Wealthy Believe They Will Be Someday,"
LendingTree, October 9, 2023, https://www.lendingtree.com/debt
-consolidation/wealth-survey/#:~:text=With%20more%20time%
20to%20make,percentage%20points%20from%20last%20year.

13 According to Kasser's research, for materialists "unhappiness comes
from not getting what they wanted or getting what they want and
discovering that its empty. Often materialists' goals are false or inflated:
they think rich people are smart and happy and they see themselves as
falling short. Of course, media is a primary cause of these false goals,
and materialistic people watch a lot of TV." Tim Kasser, *The High Price
of Materialism*, (Cambridge, MA: MIT Press, 2003).

14 Andrews, *Slow Is Beautiful*, 23.

15 "When we are unhappy or unfulfilled, we often cling to money even
more. . . . Materialism sucks you into a debilitating vortex: pursuing
money makes you materialistic; materialism reduces your well-being,
so you grasp even harder for power and money, putting you more
deeply into the unsatisfying clutches of materialism." Andrews,
Slow Is Beautiful, 55.

16 Ron Marshall, "How Many Ads Do You See in One Day?," *Red Crow
Marketing*, September, 10, 2015, https://www.redcrowmarketing.
com/2015/09/10/many-ads-see-one-day/. In the 1970s, Americans saw
an average of 500 ads per day. Caitlin Johnson, "Cutting Through
Advertising Clutter," CBS News *Sunday Morning*, Sept. 17, 2006,
https://www.cbsnews.com/news/cutting-through-advertising-clutter/.

17 Hari, *Lost Connections*, 100, citing Neal Lawson, *All Consuming:
How Shopping Got Us into This Mess and How We Can Find Our Way
Out* (London: Penguin, 2009), 143; and Martin Lindstrom, *Brandwashed:
Tricks Companies Use to Manipulate Our Minds and Persuade Us to Buy*
(New York: Kogan Page, 2012), 10.

18 This pendulum is inspired by the Communities United Against
Violence (CUAV) "Gems of Change" poster series, and it inspired
the other pendulum images in this book. You can see the posters at:
https://www.facebook.com/media/set/?set=a.10154100712872646
.1073741844.136985472645&type=3.

19 Sylvia Federicci, interview in Nick Montgomery and carla bergman's *Joyful Militancy: Building Thriving Resistance in Toxic Times* (Chico, CA: AK Press, 2017), 61: "It means that . . . you understand the situation, and you're active in a way that you feel that you are comprehending and moving along in accordance to what is required in that moment. So you feel that you have the power to change and you feel yourself changing with what you're doing, together with other people. It's not a form of acquiescence to what exists."

20 Montgomery and bergman insightfully argue that dominant systems need to "constantly crush and subdue the forces of transformation. They do not merely need obedience; they need their subjects to be separated from their own capacities," in *Joyful Militancy*, 51.

21 Some of the teachers I have learned these ideas from include: Prentis Hemphill, B Stepp, Arinna Weisman, Staci Haines, Nathan Shara, Lisa Thomas-Adeyemo, and adrienne maree brown.

22 Johann Hari, *Stolen Focus: Why You Can't Pay Attention—and How to Think Deeply Again* (New York, NY: Crown, 2022).

23 Charles Duhig, *The Power of Habit: Why We Do What We Do in Life and Business* (New York, NY: Random House, 2014).

24 Samuel P. L. Veissière and Moriah Stendel, "Hypernatural Monitoring: A Social Rehearsal Account of Smartphone Addiction," *Frontiers in Psychology*, vol. 9, 2018, https://doi.org/10.3389/fpsyg.2018.00141.

25 Judith Butler, *Gender Trouble: Feminism and the Subversion of Identity* (New York, NY: Routledge, 2006).

Chapter Two: Stuck on Autopilot: Swinging between Numbness and Big Feelings

1 Hari, *Lost Connections*, 40.

2 Francis Weller, *The Wild Edge of Sorrow: Rituals of Renewal and the Sacred Work of Grief* (Berkeley, CA: North Atlantic Books, 2015), 404.

3 Ibid., 363.

4 Ibid., 215.

5 Andrews, *Slow Is Beautiful*, 184.

6 Weller, *Wild Edge of Sorrow*, 238.

7 Ibid., 278.

8 Ibid., 233

9 Jessica Fern, *Polywise: A Deeper Dive into Navigating Open Relationships* (Canada: Thornapple Press, 2023).

Chapter Three: Falling in Love and Losing Your Mind: The Romance Cycle

1 One of the classics in the relationship self-help genre is Harville Hendrix's *Getting the Love You Want: A Guide for Couples* (New York, NY: HarperPerennial, 1988). This book has many of the pitfalls of the genre, but there are some very useful insights in it about why romantic relationships stir up such strong feelings and so much conflict. This section pulls many of Hendrix's insights into a more politicized framework that can be of use to those who want to get free of the romance myth's illusions.

2 Hendrix, *Getting the Love You Want*, 14, 36.

3 Ibid., 45.

4 Hendrix, *Getting the Love You Want*, 44.

5 Ibid., 50–52.

6 Ibid., 60.

7 Ibid., 53.

8 Ibid., 25–27.

9 Ibid., 24.

10 Ibid., 30.

11 Ibid.

12 Ibid., 32. Hendrix says these are "those parts of our false self that are too painful to acknowledge."

13 Ibid., 33.

14 Ibid., 64–67.

15 Ibid., 80.

16 Ibid., 20.

17 Ibid., 75.

18 Ibid., 79.

19 Ibid., 72–73.

20 Ibid., 62.

21 This exercise is inspired by Harville Hendrix's description of a "reromanticizing exercise" in *Getting the Love You Want*, 163.

Chapter Four: Encountering Fear, and the Courage to Say Yes and No

1 David Richo, *How to Be an Adult: A Handbook for Psychological and Spiritual Integration* (Boston: Shambhala Pub., 2002), 66–67.

2 Ibid. This is similar to something that Nathan Shara taught in a Generative Somatics course I attended in 2018. He said, "We are all still dependent on other people to live, but it's no longer any one person's obligation to meet our needs." Many of us treat people in our lives, especially romantic partners, as if they were a parent obligated to meet our needs, and we feel resentment or anger if they fail to do so, as if it were their responsibility. The romance myth feeds this illusion. More freedom and choice are available when we recognize that we can ask another adult for some kind of support, they can say yes or no, and we can make choices about seeking it from others or from ourselves if they say no.

3 Richo, *How to Be an Adult*, 68.

4 Ibid., 69.

5 Ibid., 49–50.

6 Ibid.

7 Mia Mingus, "Interdependency (excerpts from several talks)," *Leaving Evidence*, blog, January 22, 2010, https://leavingevidence.wordpress.com /2010/01/22/interdependency-exerpts-from-several-talks/.

8 Johnson, *Hold Me Tight*, 36.

9 Ibid., 31.

10 Ibid., 52.

11 These statements are inspired by a list that Johnson provides. Ibid., 81–82.

12 See Richo, *How to Be an Adult*, for a useful chart that goes more deeply into this inquiry, 59.

13 Cristien Storm, *Empowered Boundaries: Speaking Truth, Setting Boundaries, and Inspiring Social Change* (Berkeley, CA: North Atlantic Books, 2018), 3–4.

14 This list is inspired by David Richo's "Characteristics of Adult Relationships" list. *How to Be an Adult*, 83.

15 Inspired by Richo's list of "Health Relationships Benchmarks." See Ibid., 65–66. See also Pia Mellody, *Facing Love Addiction: Giving Yourself the Power to Change the Way You Love* (San Francisco: HarperOne, 2003).

16 Cristien Storm, *Empowered Boundaries*, 2.

Chapter Five: What Are We Fighting About?: Communication and Repair

1 Sue Johnson, *Hold Me Tight*, 105.

2 Ibid.

3 Weyam Ghadbian and Jovida Ross use the framing of these behaviors undermining trust in their excellent conflict workbook for people in all kinds of relationships, *Turning Towards Each Other: A Conflict Workbook*, 2020 https://96cd8e90-7f87-4399-af6b-c7156e91189a.filesusr.com/ugd/05f4b7_cec53ab03dcd4f32b1fecaf66ede2d80.pdf, 22.

4 Marshall Rosenberg, *Nonviolent Communication: A Language for Life* (Encinitas, CA: Puddledancer Press, 2003).

5 If you are new to critiques of "nonviolence" and pacifism, I recommend Peter Gelderloos's book *How Nonviolence Protects the State* (Boston, MA: South End Press, 2007) as a quick, example-packed resource on how the argument that all resistance should be nonviolent is racist, sexist, and makes resistance unlikely to be effective. You can find this book online for free at The Anarchist Library, https://theanarchistlibrary.org/library/peter-gelderloos-how-nonviolence-protects-the-state.

6 Johnson, *Hold Me Tight*, 177–81. I also recommend Mia Mingus's essay, "The Four Parts of Accountability and How to Give a Good Apology," *Leaving Evidence* blog, Dec. 18, 2019, https://leavingevidence.wordpress.com/2019/12/18/how-to-give-a-good-apology-part-1-the-four-parts-of-accountability/.

7 These are inspired by ideas in Sue Johnson's book *Hold Me Tight*, 211–12.

8 I have adapted Johnson's suggestions here.

9 Ibid., 219.

Chapter Six: Revolutionary Promiscuity— Getting Free Together

1 These cultural messages are not unique to the US, though they are particularly sharp and necessary to the sustained violence and inequality upon which US economic and social relations rely. I would argue that any place organized to have prisons, a military, police, and a border, which is most places on the planet right now, cultivates these qualities and ideas at least somewhat. And many places also receive these messages directly from US imperialism via US military presence and US media presence or get direct funding from the US to build this kind of military, prison, and police infrastructure.

2 Reid Mihalko, "Reid's Slut Protocols!" https://s3.amazonaws.com/free-reid-stuff/Slut+Protocols/Slut+Protocols+Checklist+DOWNLOAD.pdf.

3 See Jessica Fern, *Polywise*.

4 I learned this question from studying with Generative Somatics. https://generativesomatics.org/.

5 Some of the language in this section was adapted from my article "Climate Disaster Is Here—and the State Will Never Save Us," *In These Times*, November 1, 2023. https://inthesetimes.com/article/climate-disaster-ecological-crisis-deluge-ministry-markley-robinson-gelderloos.

© Stephen Anunson

Dean Spade is the author of *Normal Life: Administrative Violence, Critical Trans Politics, and the Limits of Law* and *Mutual Aid: Building Solidarity During This Crisis (and the Next)*. He has worked for twenty-five years as a leading voice for trans liberation, prison abolition, and mutual aid, and has been interviewed by Bloomberg TV, *Democracy Now!*, the *Nation*, the *Getting Curious with Jonathan Van Ness* podcast, and countless other media outlets. He teaches at the Seattle University School of Law. Find him at deanspade.net.